Justin Stares is a Brussels-based journalist who before settling in Belgium lived and worked in Italy, Brazil, Argentina and the UK.

The Moon at the Bottom of the Well

Justin Stares

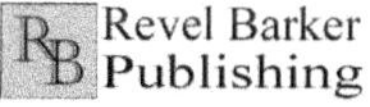

First published by Revel Barker Publishing, 2010

ISBN: 978-0-9563686-5-2

Revel Barker Publishing
66 Florence Road
Brighton BN2 6DJ
England

revelbarker@gmail.com

In memory of Derek Wilson
and with thanks to John Wilson, my parents and Bertha
for their advice and support

Part One

Ennio held one of his Nikons in one hand and wiped the lens with a tissue. He smiled, thinking back to the first camera he'd owned, the old Praktica Derek had given him, back in Israel, a real clunky machine.

The images of terrorist suspects, blindfolded, hands tied behind their backs, sitting in the dirt of the Gaza strip while waiting to be interrogated, had been the first he had ever sold – to Agence France Presse – ninety francs for six snaps. He didn't even know which buttons to press before Derek showed him. 'Some people make a living out of it, you know,' Derek had said.

That was 1967, the year Derek was sent to cover the aftermath of the Six Day War. Ennio's smile widened further at the memory of the Israeli soldiers walking around like superheroes, covered in the flowers thrown by people in the street.

As he jogged down the stairs of the Phnom Penh hotel, his mind flicked on to other images: burned-out Egyptian tanks along the invasion route near the Canal; overturned ambulances. His smile then loosened at the memory of the children in the refugee camps. He zoomed in on their desperate, ignorant faces looking out from behind the barbed wire. Some were trying to dig their way out with their bare hands.

That was just four years ago, he realised as he snapped back to the present, shaking his head in amazement at his own ascension. He gave his Nikon a final inspection, blowing on it to remove any dust. Now look at him. According to his rough calculations, the money he had earned since arriving in Saigon was enough to buy a small farm back in Italy.

He had become someone: a famous war photographer. If you were in the business, you'd sure have heard the name Ennio Iacubucci by now. The thought made him chuckle as he strode confidently through the hotel lobby. He was a solo agent now, a real photographic gun-for-hire. Long gone were the days when he had to shadow the more experienced correspondents, when the sound of gunshot made him cower in the footwell of the press car.

Phnom Penh was far grander than Saigon, Derek had said. Ennio, who in comparison had been nowhere and seen nothing, decided he agreed. He knew the Cambodian capital had three rivers and was organised into neat little partitions. On the map he had studied the layout of the Parisian tree-lined boulevards. He had walked the smart riverside promenade with its white-painted colonial villas.

He had also come to appreciate the royal palace, the gravy-boat pagodas encrusted with precious stones and the Temple of the Emerald Buddha. Unlike Saigon, Phnom Penh was spread out and always seemed empty. The only traces of war in the city were a few sandbagged public buildings and the easy-going military spokesman, whose name – Am Rong – always had the newly arrived British correspondents in stitches.

Pushing through the hotel door, he added another sign of war to the list. He was hit by the acid-like stench coming from the unused hotel pool, a reminder that war correspondents, not tourists, were now in residence.

Breathing only through his mouth, he searched for his hired mini-moke, threw his kit in the back, fired her up and within minutes was on the main road heading out of the city towards Kampong Som.

Covering Cambodia was a pain, he thought, as the wind toyed with the shoulder-length hair he groomed daily, like any self-respecting Italian.

Unlike Vietnam, in Cambodia you had no idea whose territory you were heading into. The battle lines between the Cambodians, the North Vietnamese and the Khmer Rouge were impossible to keep track of. One day you would be at a government post thirty kilometres from the capital and would be told the fighting was another thirty kilometres away. The next day that same government post would be in the hands of the North Vietnamese, and the following day back in Cambodian hands. No-one knew what was going on. How was he supposed to describe this chaos in pictures? He swerved around the potholes knowing that, somehow, it was his job to do exactly that.

At about the thirty-click mark from the city he was waved down by soldiers at a roadblock. He wasn't sure which side they were on but presumed they were North Vietnamese, who by this time were in control of most of the countryside. From underneath their pith helmets the soldiers pointed rifles at the mini-moke's windscreen. Ennio stopped, not unduly alarmed, raised his hands and smiled. He considered his smile his secret weapon. It had extricated him from innumerable scrapes.

But this time, things turned sour. Rummaging around in the vehicle, a soldier found the cameras and held them up by the straps to his comrades, talking excitedly.

'Je suis journaliste! Journaliste!' said Ennio with a little annoyance. He went for the passport in his back pocket, but this brusque movement spooked the soldier, who dropped the cameras and levelled his rifle at Ennio's head.

'No problem, no problem,' said Ennio, calmly and in English this time, raising his hands again and waving them slowly, up and down, palms down, in an attempt to placate the young boy. He was almost sure now that he had come across North Vietnamese, six of them in all.

The soldier grabbed his elbow and yanked him roughly onto the ground, nearly toppling the mini-moke in the process. Two other soldiers were soon standing over him. All three were talking at the same time.

Bloody hell. Ennio knew he couldn't negotiate lying on his arse, so he drew himself to his knees and made to get up. If he could only show them his passport and journalist's accreditation, he thought, they would understand why he was there.

The first soldier hit him sharply on the head with a rifle butt. A white light filled his vision and he slouched back to the ground, holding his head in both hands, the first trickle of blood already falling from behind his ear. Within two minutes, his situation had changed dramatically. Despite having survived many near-death situations, he was scared.

As he lay there struggling with the pain, the soldiers' quick-fire chatter went on above him. After what was probably no more than a long-lasting minute they dragged him to his feet and pushed him towards the mini-moke. For a brief moment his heart lifted: would they send him back up the road whence he came? No such luck. They took off his belt and threaded it through the front of his trousers and then through a bar at the back of the moke. His hands were tied behind his back.

Oh Jesus. He realised what was about to happen. The same soldier, whom Ennio thought must have been nineteen, got into the mini-moke and turned the engine over. After a few more shouted exchanges over the engine noise with his comrades, he began to chug away, forcing Ennio to jog behind him. Four of the soldiers stayed at the roadblock while one grabbed a bicycle that had been lying on the ground and rode alongside. He was, he realised with a depressed sigh, a prisoner.

All the time you are so sure you will get through the war alive, and here you are about to get your head chopped off. The mini-moke pulled him further and further into the countryside.

He tried laughing at his ridiculousness. Tied to a bloody mini-moke! What would the other journalists say? He couldn't believe that a routine outing had ever gone so wrong so quickly. He hoped that whenever he got wherever he was going he would meet someone senior enough, an officer hopefully, and one who spoke some European language, who would appreciate that war correspondents were impartial observers. As things stood he knew they suspected he was a spy.

The further out into the country they got, the more his heart sank. The fields rolled by kilometre after kilometre while civilisation, at least in the form of Phnom Penh, receded. By the time they turned off the road onto a dirt track he calculated he had been jogging for about an hour, perhaps eight kilometres. Fortunately he was physically fit; they hadn't let him stop for a minute.

The road ran down into a shaded grove and approached some flimsy looking tin-roofed huts beneath palm tress. Out of the huts and from the surrounding fields men started to appear, some carrying sickles. They asked questions of the soldiers, who gave them one-sentence answers.

A farmer approached Ennio, got really close and spat in his face. '*Sale americain!*' he hissed: dirty American. Another approached, raising his sickle as if to strike Ennio in the head before holding back, laughing at the fear on Ennio's face and repeating: *'sale americain!'*

More men came.

'*Non! Je suis italien*!' Ennio cried. 'Italian!' No-one seemed to hear. As their numbers increased, a mass hysteria seemed to take hold of the villagers. They began to argue furiously among themselves, breaking off only to spit on their prisoner. One of them delivered a resounding slap then punches began to rain down.

Inside the village, the soldiers calmly dismounted, instructed Ennio to kneel and began talking with the village men, throwing dirty glances from time to time at their prisoner. This was it, he thought. They were going to torture him and kill him. The expectation of pain made him hyperventilate and tremble.

As if to confirm his worst fears, a man appeared with a rope. Were they going to hang him? He shouted out: *'Laissez-moi expliquer.'* Let me explain. They ignored him.

The man with the rope laced it under his arms and around his shoulders and back onto the mini-moke. As he tested the tension, approving with a nod, Ennio realised they were going to drag him around. His first reaction was one of relief that he would avoid the hangman's noose, at least for the moment, but this was quickly replaced by dread of the injuries he almost certainly now faced. He had seen many open, festering, wounds before. He knew there would be no medical treatment. And he suspected this would in any case be just the first round of torture.

The soldier got back on the moke and began to drive away. Ennio tried desperately to keep up by running but fell within seconds. This time, he was on his backside, head towards the moke, feet trailing. The driver revved up some speed and began to circle inside the makeshift village square. Pebbles immediately scraped the skin from Ennio's back. His head bashed up and down mercilessly against the dirt. Harder every time. After maybe thirty seconds he could feel a warm intense pain from the friction burns to his legs. A warning a motorcycle instructor had given him years before came to mind: 'Your head is a melon. If the skin bursts the insides will all come gushing out, so wear a helmet.'

He heard laughter. What now? After another sharp jolt and bright white light, he passed out.

The first thing he felt when he came to was something tickling his nose. A long blade of grass had lodged itself right inside the nostril. He started to move his hand towards his head to dislodge it when the pain kicked in. It felt as if his head had swollen to twice its size. To move it even slightly in any direction involved an intense throbbing. No sooner had his hand reached his head than pain kicked in from elsewhere: his leg. The ride around the square had left his jeans torn in many places. Below both knees his legs were stained blood-red, but the pain was coming from higher up: his backside, more precisely the right cheek of his backside. He tentatively prodded it with a finger and discovered with an equal measure of horror and repulsion that the cheek, entirely exposed, was no longer smooth. Chunks seemed to be missing.

With the one eye he could open, he looked around: it looked and smelt like a barn. Braced against the good leg, he tried to raise himself, and heard rattling, the chains. He was chained to a wooden twin-oxen yoke in the corner of a barn. Happy to be alive, he lay back down. He was thirsty.

He must have passed out again or slept, because the next thing he knew it was raining. At first he imagined it to be a dream, but then he was sure he felt a steady flow. Pretty drops pattered on his head. Water! But how could it be raining inside a barn? Oddly, only his face seemed to be getting wet. He opened his good eye and was about to open he mouth too when he saw someone moving, heard new laughter, and smelt something vaguely acidic, as if he were back by the hotel pool. Fuck, he thought, and turned his head away. Somebody was pissing on him.

When the first session was finished, the second began. Two men, or maybe boys. Before the pair left, they gave him a couple of kicks in the arse, right on the open wound. Struggling but failing to suppress the pain, Ennio started to sink into a deep, dark depression. This was, he was sure, the start of a long, drawn-out death.

Night began to fall. While he could still see anything, Ennio finished inspecting himself. He was, he concluded, unlikely to die of the wounds he had already picked up, though there was a fair chance that his leg – his arse – would quickly become infected. He was chained to the yoke by one arm and one leg. With his free hand he went through his shirt pockets: only tissues were left. Only one pocket remained of his jeans. In it, he found his passport. The front page was half missing, but it was largely intact. So his Italian passport had finally come in handy – it had saved his left arse cheek. His Italian nationality had been a hindrance for most of his adult life (as a child he'd never given it any thought) but since arriving in Asia he saw that there were in fact worse nationalities to have. Like Vietnamese.

He threw the passport to the ground and lay back down. He tried to sleep despite his desperate thirst. He couldn't. Nausea added itself to his list of ailments.

The next morning the boys were back to piss on him, three of them this time. One, whose large forehead and rotting teeth made him look retarded, drew a knife from his belt when he had finished. The dirty blade triggered a new bout of hyperventilation. The boy knelt on his chest, whispering to him, passing the knife behind his ear. With a sharp, sudden movement, a mesh of hair and skin was separated from the scalp. He held the clump up to his friend, laughing inanely. 'Bye bye, you're dead,' said one of the other boys.

When they were gone, Ennio wept out of self-pity. Rather than a sob it was a wail, its tone rising and falling as if it were a song. His mind left his body and looked down from close by. The mind was listening, analysing the tune. The mind was puzzled. What song was Ennio humming? Could it possibly be Cavaradossi's aria from *Tosca*? How did that go? Yes, he could remember it now. The analysis complete, the external mind collapsed back into its head.

Running through the aria helped soothe his fear. He hummed it, whistled it and even broke out into a croaky song. Cavaradossi... the melody flowed like water, like a river, unstoppable, without beginning or end, fluid... water... a river... the Liri. He pictured the Liri. Where did it start? In the Abruzzo mountains? In the lake? How much of its course had he walked?

There was that time they'd sunbathed in the dried-up riverbed; Derek always wanted to sunbathe naked, the little pervert. The Liri... the Abruzzo... Morrea... my village... my mother...

He bored down into his past, focusing like the wrong end of a telescopic lens on some immutable, inner core. How far back could he go? What were they thinking on the day he was born?

*

Morrea. A godforsaken place so far off the beaten track that not even the eagles know where it is. Snow is falling on December 9 1940; it's Mussolini's era. It's a national holiday. Relatives gather downstairs to celebrate the birth. A baby; a boy, thank the Lord, has come into the world. He is wrapped tightly to ensure he grows up strong and healthy.

A bastard, but what can you do? Mother is not going to tell anybody who the father is. She seems to delight in her little secret. The only clue she will give is that the man lives in the village.

Poverty. Not enough food. Illiteracy. Most villagers sign their name with a cross.

Pride. Too proud to beg. So how do you get enough to eat? It's simple; you work the fields.

Before he is even born, Ennio is separated from his father. The separation from his mother begins soon afterwards.

Initially, it's not intentional. While his mother works, Ennio the toddler is left alone. She thinks he can't come to much harm, the foolish woman.

But inevitably, one day she returns to find he has turned their tiny house upside down. 'You're a little wretch!' she screams, pinching his cheeks. Ennio laughs; the pinches don't hurt. This makes her even more angry. She hits him hard, making him cry.

It's Italy after all; a typical, hysterical mother-and-son relationship. Guilty now, mother ceases beating. 'Are you hungry you little wretch?' Two is not much of a family, but they have family meals all the same. Ennio the toddler throws more food on the floor than he eats.

There is no male figure, no-one to inject balance into their lives. They love each other to bits and drive each other up the wall at the same time, every day.

The problem, of course, does not go away. How can you work and take care of your baby?

It happens again. Back from work, mother sees Ennio the four-year-old bleeding from a head wound. 'Where have you been?' she screams.

'Here all the time,' he says. She looks in horror at the gaping gash. She keeps screaming: 'What happened? What happened?' He is too young to answer, or at least to explain. To the doctor's; a three-kilometre walk. Italy at its most backward. No buses, not even a road, just a dirt track. If you have heavy loads to transport, you use a mule.

Ennio recovers, thanks to the doctor, in twenty days. Mother realises she can't leave him alone. Wherever she goes, he has to come. If she's working the fields, he sits there, playing in the dirt. There's a new problem: Ennio wanders off as soon as she turns her back.

A few months later, they write to mother from the town hall telling her to go in person to sort out some bureaucracy. Ennio is shipped off to his aunt's for the duration.

After lunch, the aunt tells the boy: 'I'm going out to feed the pigs. You stay here, you understand? Don't leave the house, because outside there are wolves.'

'What are wolves?'

'They're animals that eat naughty children.'

The fright tactics are enough to stop him leaving the house, but not enough to keep him out of trouble. By the time aunt comes back Ennio has hit his head yet again and passed out, falling into the fireplace. Only two days later does he recover consciousness. The scars from this little incident will never fade completely.

On her return, seeing the state he's in, his mother also passes out. She blames it on herself. 'I will never leave you alone again,' she swears, covering him with oil for the burns, then with kisses. Who would have thought that a few years later she would abandon him like an unwanted dog?

But that is later. In the meantime, during Ennio's bandage-covered recuperation, there is a more pleasant experience; he earns his first kiss, from his cousin Laura.

No sooner is he able to get out of bed than there she is, knocking at the door, dressed in pink, pure, smiling. She is a few years older than Ennio, but they have grown up together.

‘I was on my way to church and I thought I would make a little detour to see how you were,’ she says.

‘I’m very happy to see you as I’ve been in bed for three days and I haven’t talked to anybody,’ he tells her, rising like a *signorino* to make her coffee.

‘No, let me,’ she says, beating him to the kitchen and making coffee herself.

They talk of the village children’s preferred game: hide and seek. If a boy is seeking and he finds another boy, nothing happens, but if a boy finds a girl, he can demand a kiss.

Ennio is fond of this rule and gains the confidence necessary to enforce it by the age of five. Hide and seek is the perfect training ground for the adolescent dating that would come. The girls are taught that once the game is over, they have to put out.

Laura brings Ennio up to speed on the village gossip. They play cards and generally have a pleasant time. The next day she comes back like the well educated girl she is to say hello to mother, and then the next day after that, and then every day until Ennio recovers.

Soon after he is fully fit, they are back to playing hide and seek. He finds her, and really kisses her, grabbing her head in both hands. He is developing a taste for girls, especially for slim, petite girls.

Time to start attending school. Infant school. Ennio gets to play with toy bricks and to draw. According to the teacher’s reports, he is a bright boy, a quick learner.

He needs to go to junior school, the teacher says, but because there isn’t one in the village, this means sending Ennio to a boarding school or ‘college,’ a word that for him will always be synonymous with anger and fear. It’s in Aquila, the nearest town.

Mother goes to the town hall where they give her the appropriate forms to fill in. A cross marks her assent. Her son is not told what lies in store.

On the first day, Ennio doesn’t want to be separated from ‘mamma’ and cries for an hour when she says she is going back without him. He is inconsolable so she changes her tune.

‘Don’t worry, mamma won’t leave you,’ she says.

‘Are you telling the truth?’

‘Yes, I’m staying here with you,’ she lies.

But then a little sod comes up and asks: 'What are you doing here? Have you come to board with us?'

'No,' Ennio says, 'my mother has come to talk with someone, and as soon as she has finished we are leaving.'

'You haven't got it yet, have you?' the boy says. 'Your mother is sending you away to college.'

At the word 'college' Ennio flings his arms around his mother's legs. 'I don't want to live here,' he tells her. 'I want to stay with you.'

'But this isn't a college,' she says.

'Yes it is, and you want to leave me here.'

'No, it's not,' she insists.

'Really?' he says, at which she smiles in the knowledge that she can still hoodwink him if she tries hard enough.

Ennio calls the snotty-nosed boy over and asks him in front of his mother: 'What is this building?'

'It's a college,' the boy repeats, but mother, a competent liar, won't admit it even then.

'That boy is mistaken,' she says.

'Well mistaken or not, I'm hungry and I want to leave,' Ennio tells her. Right on cue, a nun comes out of the building and says: 'Why don't you come in and have *minestra* with us?'

'I'm only coming if mamma comes too,' Ennio says.

'Ok mamma, you come too,' says the nun. Mother and son follow her into a big canteen.

The *minestra* looks good but Ennio is prevented from picking up his spoon and told to say the Lord's Prayer. 'If you don't say it, you can't eat,' says the nun.

'But I don't know it,' he says.

'It goes like this,' says the nun. Soon, tired of repeating after her, he takes up his spoon again.

'No, no,' says the nun. 'If you don't say it you can't eat.'

All the messing about robs Ennio of his appetite.

'Right, then, I won't,' he says, getting up to go outside. The nun grabs his arm: 'Don't worry, just eat.'

'At last! Food!' the cheeky monkey says, sitting back down to gobble.

After lunch mother says she is going to the village to buy biscuits, telling him she will be straight back. 'I want to come with you,' says Ennio.

'But it's quite a long way away,' she warns him.

'That's fine, I feel like a walk,' he says. Seeing that this ruse has failed, she drops the idea and stays put for a few minutes more. But no sooner does Ennio turn his back to play with the other boys than she is gone. It takes him about ten minutes to notice.

Running to the college gate, he cries 'Mamma! Mamma!' She isn't there. He steps forward into the street, determined to follow his mother all the way back to Morrea if he has to, but a nun grabs him from behind. He wriggles, trying to break free, still sobbing, but is physically restrained by two fibrous arms. In the distance he sees his mother disappear. She turns around once to make sure she is not being followed, and is gone.

Whom else is Ennio supposed to love? He never had a father. How can you love anybody else if you don't love your mother?

For the first few days at college he cries and doesn't eat, much to the concern of the nuns. 'What's wrong with you?' they ask.

'I miss mamma,' he shouts.

'Don't worry, she'll come and visit you every month, I'm sure,' one nun says, calmingly.

Within a few days, he gets to know everybody, and before long is playing and studying like the others, comforted in the knowledge that mother will soon return.

But she doesn't.

After a few weeks Ennio is reduced to tears by the sight of other parents coming to see their happy children. He sits in the playground alone. 'What have you done to her to make her stay away?' his new friends joke, at first. But when they see it is no laughing matter, they take a more reassuring tack: 'Don't worry, she'll be here soon.'

He begins to consider himself the son of nobody, an orphan. Whenever he cries, his friends crowd around him, each one trying to soothe him, to reassure him.

He is six years old, and is experiencing abandonment for the first time.

The period immediately after dinner is especially difficult, as this is when the post is handed out. His early hopes of a special delivery are soon dashed and Ennio resigns himself to never receiving a letter. He doesn't appreciate his mother's illiteracy. To distract himself he gets down from the table and takes a walk in the courtyard. He wonders whether his mother might have died.

Then one day she writes. 'My darling Ennio,' the letter reads, though obviously he cannot recognise the handwriting. It must be the neighbour's. 'I'm sorry I haven't been able to visit you, it's just that it has been raining so hard here I haven't been able to leave the village.'

This seems a pathetic excuse, and indeed it is. The rain does make the tracks impassable, but not for months on end. Nevertheless, the mere fact that she makes contact (plus the small amount of money she sends) is enough to plug the boy's tear ducts.

The college resembles a prison, and Ennio soon considers himself an inmate. It is a huge old building on two floors, with the nuns living on the top floor and the boarders below.

It does have its advantages. It is a few kilometres outside town and surrounded by cornfields, which in summer become the perfect playground, speckled with peach trees and cherry trees. The countryside is in fact so beautiful that tourists come from afar to visit, especially those on the way to climb the Gran Sasso.

If in summer it is bearable, winter on the other hand is awfully depressing. Life becomes unnaturally cold, humid and barren. It even bloody snows – great for a couple of days' worth of snowball fights but then such a bore.

Bird traps are the only highlight of Ennio's first winter as a boarder; he makes them from piano strings. It's quite a profitable invention as it becomes fashionable throughout the school to catch birds using crumbs lodged in a loop of wire hidden under the snow. He makes dozens, pocketing quite a few lire. Then two of his friends look over his shoulder. Before long there are more traps than birds.

Despite having received just one letter, that first year is actually a happy one compared to what is to come. Play keeps Ennio so busy he doesn't notice Christmas creeping up. Only when it is upon him does he realise December 24 is no ordinary day.

Not knowing what to do he takes a walk out of the college, along the road to a big square with an imposing panorama of the entire village and the roads leading up to it. He notices three people coming in his direction. Two are recognisable as women but the shape of the third was unclear. He waits until they are around five hundred metres away, and then sees her: Mother.

A minute later he has his arms around her neck and is shouting 'Mamma! Mamma!' Kissing her, he notices she too is crying.

'How are you doing little one?' she asks. Not wanting to start a conversation with a complaint, he tells her all is well.

'Good for you,' she says, kissing him harder than before. 'I've brought you a Christmas present!'

Taking the suitcase right out of her hand, Ennio leads his mother impatiently back towards the college. It's a heavy load for a six-year-old and he has to stop every hundred metres for a rest. 'If you can't manage let me carry it,' his mother says. By the time they get to the college entrance he is exhausted but pretends it has been a breeze. His euphoria-fuelled arms could have managed twice the weight.

A nun opens the front door. 'Couldn't you have gone round to the back door?' she asks.

'Has he behaved himself?' mother asks. 'Has he been doing all his homework?' From her face Ennio can see the nun doesn't know how to respond. He puts on his best smile, a pleading smile. He fears that without a positive report, his Christmas present will go up in smoke.

'Yes, he has behaved himself,' the nun says after a pause. Mother is content.

'If I give you your present you have to promise to behave like a decent young man,' she tells him.

The nun adds: 'The only complaint we have as far as young Ennio is concerned is that he made dozens of traps out of wires to kill birds.' She goes off on a speech about how even the birds have a right to live. 'We shouldn't kill anything living,' she says.

Ennio pretends to regret his actions, promises not to kill again. Even mother wades in: 'Such a shame to kill animals.'

'All right, all right, I won't do it again,' Ennio says, frustrated at having to repeat himself and wanting to get on with the present-opening.

'You see,' the nun says to mother. 'It's difficult to say anything to him because he gets angry straight away. He has a short fuse. He has to understand that certain things are said for his own good, but he doesn't want to know and when he gets around to regretting something it's already too late.'

This sets mother off on a speech about how children should listen to grown-ups because adults always know better. He has to stand there and take another lesson in morality before he can finally open the suitcase. In it, he finds a rich selection of food and clothes, a nice stash. Before he can finish going through the bundle the nun says it's time to go and eat with the other children. Mother eats with the nuns. They meet afterwards in the courtyard to compare meals, Italy's favourite pastime. Then she says: 'I can't stay. I have to go now or I will miss the bus.'

'Can I go with mamma to the bus-stop?' Ennio asks the nun, rushing through the door before she has a chance to answer.

'You have to behave, do you understand? If you don't behave I won't come back to visit you,' mother says on the road back to the square.

He makes all the requisite promises about behaving, studying hard and doing all his homework. 'Let's hope you are telling the truth,' she says. 'I'm making a lot of sacrifices for you to be here. It costs a lot of money. It's very hard for me. It would make me sad to think it had all gone to waste.' He promises, swears, to knuckle down. He kisses her on each cheek as she gets on the bus.

'When are you coming back to visit me?' he asks.

'Next month if you are a good boy,' she says, disappearing inside. Great news; only another month to wait.

'If I know you're coming I'll study harder,' Ennio shouts after her.

He waits on the pavement and waves as the bus departs. When the reality of her absence comes flooding back, he sits on the kerb and blubbers. Strangers pass by, seeing him but saying nothing. Then his primary school friends arrive. They pull him to his feet. 'Come on, up with you,' one says. 'Don't worry about it. Why don't we go and get an ice cream?'

Ennio finds it hard to think about anything other than his mother. Even the ice cream, paid for by a friend, is of no interest.

They wander around the village and stop off at a bar for a fizzy drink. This time he pays – it is only fair. They take it easy, strolling languidly back to their common pen.

'How come you've taken all this time just to see your mother to the bus?' snaps the nun.

'I didn't feel well so I stopped off somewhere until it passed,' says Ennio. She is silent for a few moments.

'I don't believe you,' she says.

'Well if you don't believe me, it's not my fault. You don't want me to make up a lie so that you believe me, do you?'

'I'll let you get away with it this time, but next time it won't be so easy,' she says, ordering him to the homework room to learn the Christmas poem.

The next month, mother doesn't come. Or the following month, or the month after that. She writes, promises to turn up, but there is always some kind of problem; the village roads, mostly. 'Everything is clogged up with mud,' she says in some unfamiliar hand.

This he understands; but why can't she make it during the summer months either? He misses mother, but at least he has his friends.

Two years later, she has still not returned.

*

Ennio was conscious of his nightmare, but still couldn't shake himself awake. They were torturing him in his dreams too – throttling him. No, that wasn't it. They had stuffed a rag in his mouth and lodged it in with another tied around his mouth and the back of his head. They were amusing themselves by holding his nose with thumb and forefinger, trying to keep it shut as he shook his head desperately. It had become a hilarious game: see how long you can keep his nose shut. Now you try.

He thought he was about to throw up, and sat up straight, awake. There was indeed someone holding his nose, laughing. But instead of a rag, his mouth had been stuffed with something else? What was it? He knocked the hand from his nose and spat. It was rice, boiled rice.

The boy, whom he did not recognise, gestured disapprovingly towards the rice on the floor. 'We brought you rice, and look what you have done with it,' he was obviously saying. With every second word of his brief lecture, he gave Ennio a slap, a little harder every time.

Then, another voice from behind. The boy straightened up and withdrew. An old man came forward, walking slowly and deliberately. He looked wizened, wrinkled, well dressed. His movements were almost stately. Bending down a little to inspect Ennio, he sniffed and pulled back, repulsed by the smell.

'Ah yes, I smell bad,' Ennio said in Italian.

'Who are you?' said the old man, in English.

'I am journalist,' Ennio replied. 'Italian journalist.' No reaction from the old man, whom Ennio thinks might not have understood.

'Who are you? American?' the old man said again.

'No,' said Ennio, shaking his head for emphasis. 'Italian. It-a-lian.'

'No American?' the old man said.

'Look!' Ennio shouted, pointing down at his passport. 'Look.' He picked it up and handed it over. 'Italian,' he said again. The old man fingered the document, turned and walked away with it, mumbling.

Alone again, Ennio noticed that as well as rice, they had brought him a bowl of water. Suddenly desperate, he fell on the bowl, sipping from it without lifting it from the ground. Before his thirst was completely quenched he stopped himself so as to ration the vital, life-giving supply. He must save some for later, so moved on to the rice, scooping it up from the floor, chewing it methodically, each mouthful six times before swallowing.

How long had he been there, he asked himself. A day? Two days? Pus was beginning to form on the edges of the leg wound. He began examining it every hour, half expecting to see maggots.

Later that day the boys returned to piss on him. They pissed in the bowl too, poisoning what was left of his water. He drank it anyway. Hunger was now the principal problem; a deep, grinding, loud, gnawing pain.

To sleep more comfortably he tried leaning against the yoke in a sitting position. There was not enough slack in the chains to lie down properly. He embraced the yoke with both arms, sitting gingerly on his injured arse cheek. 'This time, sleep but no nightmares,' he told himself, not really caring if he died before he awoke.

*

Two years. Just the odd letter.

Frustrated to the point he believes he will explode, Ennio decides something must be done. He is totally fed up with the college and its brainwashed, monotonous nuns.

Come the summer, he works on a plan of escape. If mother wouldn't come to him, he would go to her. It turns out to be easy. By this time Ennio is a specialist in scams, escapades and cheating the system.

The college hires a coach for a day trip into the foothills, complete with picnic. At around eleven in the morning the children file three abreast down the main street to the village in a column to the improvised bus stop in front of the only bar.

Ennio's hoarded pocket money is jiggling on his hip. The bus for Aquila, he knows, leaves at half past the hour every hour from just around the corner. While his classmates get on their bus, he convinces the nun he needs to spend a penny. 'Make it quick,' she says. He wanders over to the bar.

But instead of going inside he dashes around the back, up a side alley and on to where the Aquila bus is waiting. He lies low on the seat in case anybody comes looking for him. After an hour's journey, in Aquila, the driver tells him where to take the bus to Morrea. By nightfall he has arrived there.

It takes about half an hour to walk up the beaten track towards his mother's house, and by the time he gets there night is thick around him. He knows his mother will be in bed. Not wanting to frighten her with a rude awakening, and slightly concerned by the fact that the police might be looking for him, he spends the night in a barn, sleeping on a haystack.

Upon awakening, he gets nervous. Will mother appreciate this unexpected visit? To kill time, he loiters around the village, bumping into friends, talking about life at college, pretending to be on holiday. For food that day he goes to his aunt's, who pinches his cheeks with joy upon seeing him.

'What are you doing here?' she asks.

'I've just got a few days off,' he says.

'And why are you so hungry? Haven't you eaten at home?' she

asks after seeing him devour three plates of *minestra* and three rolls in about ten minutes (as well as a couple of glasses of watered-down wine).

'Food wasn't ready yet,' he lies. 'I'll eat again when I get home.' Bidding her goodbye and thanks he makes as if he is indeed going home, but as soon as he has turned the corner he skips over the fence and heads back towards the barn, where, despite the continuing doubts about his mother's desire to see him, he has another comfortable night's sleep.

The next morning, mother is there, screaming like a banshee and on the verge of beating him up. 'Why didn't you come home?' she yells. 'The police came looking for you, you little rat. If it wasn't for your aunt I wouldn't have known you had come back.'

On the defensive and without any kind of excuse, he resorts to tears. 'Look, you're crying and I haven't even hit you yet!' she yells, dragging him back to the house by his ear. She stops off at the telephone box to tell the military police Ennio has been found unharmed.

This escapade earns him just one meal with his mother. That same day a policeman comes to take him back to college.

'Why did you run away?' the policeman asks.

'No reason,' Ennio says. He is taken down to the village and put on a bus to Aquila. The policeman talks to the driver and sends the bus on its way. In Aquila, another policeman is waiting to take him back to the goddam college. The second copper delivers a threat: 'If you run away again we'll send you to a *casa di correzione*,' a prison for children. But he can't be that angry because he buys Ennio a bag of sweets.

At college, the nun, hands on hips, is waiting at the door. 'Tonight, as punishment, you're confined to your room,' she says.

He is obliged to feign repentance, but beyond this his jailers think no more of it. In assembly however, over the following few days, Ennio is told to show himself rather than merely say 'present' when his name is read out. Mother, it turns out, is not impressed by his escapade. Ennio's friends, on the other hand, are very much in admiration. As somebody prepared to break the rules, he starts to become something of a star.

But it is only after he learns to fistfight that his star status is confirmed.

Halfway into the following term, an ugly kid looks at him the wrong way and says something about his absent mother. Ennio invites the boy into the courtyard. The two square off, still in their aprons from cookery class, while the other pupils make a circle around them, a blind to separate the peacocks from the prying nuns.

'You're so slow you won't even be able to touch my nose,' says the ugly boy. Without bothering with banter, Ennio punches him twice, hard in the face, and then knees him in the stomach as he hits the ground.

An incisive victory; an adrenalin high. But then a comedown; the little shit squeals. Detention. 'Make sure he gets well soon, because as soon as he's back on his feet he's getting some more,' Ennio tells the little shit's friend.

'You shouldn't knee people while they are on the ground,' the friend says. 'If you hadn't kneed him, you wouldn't have won the fight.' Was it an unfair fight? Who cares? When the gloves are off, there are no rules as far as Ennio is concerned.

A few days later, good to his word, he goes to the shit's dormitory to see if his swelling has gone down. 'Do you want some more?' Ennio asks. The boy makes the first move, slapping Ennio as if he were a girl. In return he gets brought down with a judo throw and kicked in the face. He bleeds all over the floor.

'Tell him that as soon as he is ready he can have some more,' Ennio says, walking nonchalantly out of the dormitory. The other boys in the dorm eye him, jaws wide open, with a mixture of fear and respect.

After this second fight, Ennio becomes the college's main man. Whatever he wants, he takes. If anyone objects, they get a kicking. Like an archetypal Italian *capo* he wanders around college with his right-hand man. The two become inseparable. Very soon everybody is terrified of him, putty in his hands. He is a big fish in a little pond, a boy respected among his peers. But not by the authorities of course; he pays for his mafia-like status with innumerable detentions. The detention room becomes his home from home.

He also gets a few hidings himself, from the older boys. But Ennio is growing and will soon be their size. They establish a truce, and then the older boys move on. In his final year, Ennio has the college to himself. He is he realises, a trainee delinquent.

The escapades continue too. There are three in all. Whenever he goes missing the police are called, and every time they find him they threaten to send him to the *casa di correzione*. They don't, of course; fighting in the playground is not a crime at the age of ten. But the police do open a file on Ennio, much to his mother's shame. She visits a little more regularly, every few months, in part to stop Ennio escaping and in part to talk him into mending his ways. She brings him sweets and cigarettes (all aspiring men smoke) and hands them over on condition that he takes school more seriously. He always promises he will.

He is, in fact, not a bad student. His subjects don't really challenge him. While he has no intention of coming top of his class, he is only once in danger of having to repeat a year; when he falls sick.

These junior school years are, all told, good years. Ennio the boy dreams of becoming a man but does not yet have to face responsibility. It is the calm before the storm.

*

No sooner had he entered his dream cycle than he was woken by the sound of the barn door opening.

He turned his head, expecting to see more village boys come to relieve themselves.

But no – he saw a girl. A young girl, perhaps ten, in a simple red dress. It was still light outside. She shut the door behind her and they both let their eyes grow accustomed to the shadow.

She stood there, leaning back on the door, looking at Ennio, not moving and not talking.

'Hello darling,' he said. 'What's your name?'

She didn't react. She just examined the prisoner with her eyes, paying particular attention to his chains and injuries.

'Come over here, sweetheart,' he said to her, motioning with one hand. 'Sit on that bucket over there.' He pointed.

She seemed to understand and headed for the bucket, her little feet treading an ellipse so as not to come too close to Ennio. Once there, she just sat and stared. No emotion was visible in her eyes.

‘What’s your name?’ said Ennio. He tried again in French: *‘Tu t’appelles comment, mon amour?’* He pointed at himself. ‘Ennio,’ he said. ‘And you?’ He pointed at her. Nothing. She just sat there staring at him.

He smiled. ‘You’re so sweet,’ he said. He tried asking for water, pointing at the bowl and his own mouth. Still no reaction.

He examined her more closely and decided that she might be older than he first imagined. She was short but there were definitely signs of breasts under her dress, and her face didn’t have that never-been-kissed look pre-pubescent girls had. She had a bit of a swerve to the hips. Maybe twelve, he thought. He counted to twelve with his one free hand and pointed at her. ‘Are you twelve?’ he asked.

Nothing but the faintest of smiles, which Ennio returned generously.

Twelve, he thought. Those little Italian whores have seen it all by the age of twelve.

*

It’s not much fun for a ten-year-old in hospital. Lying in bed means missing both play and lessons. Missing lessons, Ennio knows, could mean struggling with the end-of-year exams.

It’s his last winter in primary school, and there is some kind of nasty bug going around which he is sure he won’t get. But the cleaning ladies mess up. They switch his pillow with that of another boy who has already been hospitalised in Aquila.

As soon as he starts to feel a little off they take him to the surgery for an examination. ‘You did well to bring him here straight away,’ the doctor said. ‘The sickness hasn’t got into his head yet, so we’ll be able to cure him in a couple of weeks.’

On the second day inside they attach him to a machine and treat him with rays. He feels nothing, but soon after all his hair falls out. ‘What an ugly brute,’ he says upon seeing himself in the mirror.

The nun who doubles as nurse smothers his baldness with cream. ‘It doesn’t matter what you look like, so long as you get better,’ she says. He rebounds. Within a few days he is fighting fit again. Indeed, Ennio is soon quite bored with hospital life, though the doctors won’t let him go back to college until they are sure he is totally cured.

So to kill time he embarks on forays around the hospital.

While inside, Ennio has made a new friend, a nice lad; they agree on pretty much everything. He has one serious defect, this friend; he has ears so big they could be mistaken for sails.

The boy latches onto Ennio because Ennio won't let the other sick boys make fun of his ears. Those who don't want to understand get slapped.

After discovering every wing of the hospital, boredom entices the duo outside. They wander into the courtyard with the intention of looking for old men to make fun of.

But there aren't any; it's the cold weather, probably. The intrepid explorers therefore climb over the hospital courtyard wall and into another garden. On the other side of the lawn they see a single-storey building with a series of large windows. From far away they can see figures moving around inside. As they approach they realise they are watching a group of girls changing clothes. The window has no curtains or blinds, so it is easy to see inside. The girls are twelve or thirteen years old and are putting on their pyjamas. Several are developed enough to wear bras.

'Look how beautiful they are,' Ennio exclaims to his friend. The girls have noticed they are being spied upon. One opens the window and calls out: 'Haven't you seen a girl before?'

'Not naked,' says Ennio.

'Come around to the front and we'll let you into the bedroom.'

Until this day Ennio has had no contact with girls or women, other than the nuns. Sex is already on his mind and a topic of keen conversation in college, but no-one has actually had any. So to be propositioned in this way makes him nervous.

'I can stand here and watch you. I don't need to come around the front,' he says.

'No, no,' they reply in unison. 'Come around to the front or you won't see any more.'

They give instructions on how to get from the front door of what he supposes is a dormitory in a girls' school, to their room.

'Let's go,' Ennio says indecisively to his friend, who is terrified at the prospect and physically shaking.

'What are you scared of? We're going to see girls. We're not getting locked up,' says Ennio with false bravado. Butterflies in their stomachs, they edge their way around the building.

It takes them a while to find the right path down through the school to the dormitory which, despite overlooking the garden, is on a lower floor than the entrance. The door is locked and the boys have to shout to get let in.

'Oh, it's you two,' one of the girls says in a matter-of-fact way. 'Come in.'

Inside, Ennio avoids looking any of them in the eye. It feels wicked.

'What were you doing at the window?' one asks.

'We didn't feel like hanging around in the hospital courtyard so we went around looking for something different to do,' Ennio says, his voice trembling a little.

'And how long have you been in hospital?' another says. 'How old are you?'

He answers but the more he speaks, the more his voice begins to waver. Very soon he has trouble speaking at all. They're beautiful girls and they're only wearing pyjamas, is the one thought in his head. Two are sitting on the edge of their beds. When they bend forward their breasts almost fall out of their tops. Ennio thinks they are doing this on purpose, showing off. While he sits on a stool, enjoying the show, one girl says: 'Come on, what's wrong? Are you afraid to speak? It's not like we are going to bite you.'

'It's not you biting me that I'm afraid of – it's just that I'm on fire inside. It's consuming me.' He's quite proud of his use of the verb 'to consume'. Quite a bright ten-year-old.

'What does consume mean?' the girls ask. Ennio explains that as soon as he leaves the bedroom he will have to go to the toilet.

'And what are you going to do in the toilet?' The girls laugh. He says nothing, looks down and struggles with the nerves. He can feel his voice failing him again. 'Come on, what are you going to do in the toilet?'

He might as well come clean, he thinks: 'I'll go to the toilet to have a wank.'

'What does wank mean?'

They laugh; real teases.

Ennio falls silent, annoyed at the fun-making. They must know what it means, he thinks.

'I'll have a wank because you are beautiful girls and this is the first time that I've seen girls dressed only in pyjamas and I like you very much.'

'Come on, what is a wank?'

'It's a beautiful thing which I do because I don't have a woman of my own because I am still small,' he says.

'Are you any good at doing it?' Amid the giggles, the oestrogen rises.

'If you're not embarrassed I'll do it right here and now,' Ennio says, though hearing the words come out of his mouth makes his whole body feel light and his head dizzy.

'No, we're not afraid,' they all say. 'Go on, do it!'

Despite his nerves he has a big hard-on, so big he struggles to get it out of his trousers. The girls keep teasing: 'Come on, or are you no good at doing it?'

He pretends not to hear, but they kept on teasing: 'You're no good at doing it.'

Ennio turns away from them and towards his mate, who is laughing too, a laugh full of madness, desperation and amazement.

'You're no good!' the girls shout. Ennio is getting so annoyed he doesn't want to do it any more but at the same time realises he has to prove himself.

He opens his fly, takes it out and starts to wank, with shaking hands. He stands in the hope of achieving better balance and control, but this actually makes things worse. His head starts to spin and his feet to give way. He has to lie down. He collapses on one of the girls, who lets off a scream of both fright and pleasure. A right mess; lying there on the bed he starts to laugh at the whole situation. The laughing opens a release valve. He starts to relax.

Sitting up, he looks at the girl he has fallen on, looks her straight in the eyes, cock in hand, and tells her how beautiful she is.

'That's enough now,' she says, looking down at it with more than a little concern.

'But this is what you wanted,' Ennio protests. 'I'm just doing what you asked.'

A girl sitting on the other side of him takes it in both hands and starts wanking him off herself. He steadies himself using both arms stretched out behind him, in wonder at the unfolding events. Everyone in the room is staring at the girl's hands rubbing up and down.

After maybe twenty seconds a bit of juice squirts out, not the usual quantity, but nevertheless Ennio feels there is no more. And in any case, he now has a headache. He is, after all, not completely cured.

'I don't feel like it any more,' he says, adding, 'in any case I had a wank before I came out.'

The girls, silent by now, seem impressed with his sperm-making abilities. He stands up and puts it away.

With his mate he stays for about another fifteen minutes, chatting. The girls hand out chocolate and sweets and then start complaining they are tired. They ask the boys to leave so they can sleep.

It's dark, and it's time for dinner, so they head back over the wall and on to the dining hall where the other kids are already waiting to be served.

While downing pasta Ennio tells his big-eared friend to keep his trap shut about what they have been up to. 'If you don't, everyone will want to go,' he predicts. The friend keeps his promise despite the nagging of the other curious children.

The few remaining days in hospital are spent stealing eggs from a nearby farm, playing football in the courtyard and tormenting old people. Tormenting is the preferred pastime. One old man has holes in his arse. Another has tuberculosis and another can't walk at all. They all get taunted until they get so angry they take up their walking sticks and swing them around, too slow to catch the boys.

So they complain to the nuns, and the boys are reprimanded for being disrespectful. 'We didn't really mean to cause trouble, we were just passing the time,' they say.

They pronounce Ennio fit. Thank God. A nun picks him up and takes him back to college. He says goodbye. The boys say they will miss him because he is the only one in hospital capable of livening things up a little. 'It's a morgue in here normally,' says one long-term patient.

'Don't worry,' Ennio says. 'As soon as you're fit again we'll see each other in college.' Quite a few of his classmates are hospitalised by this time.

It is a three-week sojourn in all, and it's enough to instil Ennio with a real repulsion towards hospitals. He vows to die rather than to return. It's the walking corpses that get to him most. And the frustration; looking out of the window and seeing people who are fit and well, walking, running around and smoking, going about their lives.

*

The girl heard the door first and darted cat-like into the far corner of the barn, where she hid behind machinery.

The boys had come back, three of them, two of whom Ennio thought he recognised.

They were drunk; he smelt the alcohol on their breath from five metres away.

They approached and stood over him for a while, talking and pointing. One bent towards him and shouted, who knows what. His insults were so violent they came with spit. It wafted over and landed on Ennio's face.

The boy then lifted his foot and showing the sole to Ennio, just left it hanging in front of his face. Ennio braced, held his hand up in expectation. The foot shot forward and hit the hand. The hand hit the face. It hurt.

More chatter and then another kick to the head, with the bridge of the foot this time.

The second boy joined in. He launched himself into the air and came down on Ennio's stomach, much to the amusement of his friend.

All three then got in on the act, practicing their karate moves. Roundhouse kicks, mule kicks. One knocked Ennio's already swollen head into the yoke. A punch to the mouth dislodged a tooth. A second punch knocked the tooth out completely.

Ennio's mind went numb. He passed out again, though this time slowly, in stages, between blows. The only thought in his head was the hope that the beating would end quickly. Not once was he tempted to pray to God for help. In the corner of the room he caught a glimpse of the girl, watching.

*

That year, Ennio's last at the college, his mother doesn't visit at Christmas. She can't be well enough to travel, he thought.

The following spring and summer he has a decent teacher, and with help and encouragement he gets through his end-of-year exams.

Mother still hasn't appeared. The teacher is good enough to invite Ennio to spend the holidays with his wife at their village near Pescara. As he gambols across their lawn with the other children he has a sickly, uncomfortable feeling. Is it fear? School is over; there are no more minions to dominate. What is next?

As the holidays draw to a close, the nuns appear and tell Ennio that to continue his studies he has to go to a secondary school. He shrugs his shoulders.

One bright day in October mother superior comes to pick him up at the college. Ennio cries silently at the thought of leaving for good, conscious at the same time of the irony; he never wanted to be there in the first place. It is nevertheless a sad day.

'Keep studying and be a good boy,' mother superior says. 'Make me proud of you.'

He cries because he has been happy. It's upsetting to think he won't see any of his victim-friends again. He worries things won't be as cosy where he is going. They give him sweets for the forty-kilometre car journey from Aquila to his new, senior, boarding school. He travels with three other boys, he has the front seat. It is his first time in a car. He is eleven years old and is as educated as any other country Italian boy of his age, if not more so.

A new town, Capestrano. A small place of around two thousand residents, cute, with asphalted streets and a medieval castle in the middle of the town square surrounded by thick rows of flowers which blossomed in summer and gave off a rich, powerful scent after nightfall.

The surroundings are a definite improvement on the college, and the climate is better too; it hardly ever snows in Capestrano. The school, staffed by monks this time, is on a hill just outside the town. The building has a private lane leading up to it, lined with olive trees on both sides.

It takes Ennio and his companions about ten minutes to walk up from the town centre. The school itself looks like a church. It's difficult to find the entrance. The doors, when he does finally find them, are huge. Once inside he is greeted by a man who asks who he is and which school he has come from.

'Welcome,' he says. 'It won't take long for you to feel at home. I see you're already used to boarding. Most boarding schools work the same way.'

'Yes, I'm sure I'll fit in,' Ennio replies confidently. 'I'm not afraid of boarding. I had to board throughout my primary years because there was no primary school in the village I come from.'

The new school is immense. Around seventy boys sleep in the downstairs dormitory they call 'the arsenal'. The beds are spaced out at one-metre intervals. From the door all you can see are beds, like gravestones, stretching out towards the horizon.

The school canteen is on the same scale, as are the study rooms. To get from one room to another you have to walk quite a way, sometimes crossing the courtyard. It's a former monastery. Shortly before the war the monks ran out of money and had to set up a school to scrape together enough cash for the building repairs.

For the first few days Ennio hangs around pretty much alone. Almost all the boys are older, the eldest are fifteen, and they're not really interested in getting to know a new eleven-year-old. Some of the final-years think they are the Almighty Father Himself. Until then, *capo dei capi* has been Ennio's job. It's quite a comedown.

His loneliness does not last long however as around two weeks later, as he is sitting on a wall looking over the town, he recognises a figure walking up the lane. It's his old right-hand man, Feruccio, arriving with his father.

Seeing Feruccio cheers Ennio up no end. What a great kid; bright, passionate about school and a bit of an artist, a lover of drawing. Tall and good looking, he can boast jet-black hair (natural, not coloured) and blue-black eyes. He is something of a thinker too. Over the months to come, they will sit together under a tree, sheltering from the sun, pondering on life and what they might achieve when they grow up, if all goes well.

Feruccio is an upbeat, life-loving kid, which is good news for

Ennio, given his own downbeat mood. If Feruccio finds Ennio sitting on his own, lost in thought, he tries to snap him out of it. 'Just you try to catch me,' he says, slapping Ennio on the face playfully. The ensuing chase around the school can last for hours, as Feruccio is the faster runner. Before long they are exhausted and collapse on the ground, their heads emptied of all negativity.

Feruccio's arrival lifts Ennio's spirits tremendously. Despite the summer weather he has been moping. While the other boys have spent almost four months with their parents before arriving, he has been forced to spend the holidays with his teacher. There is still no news from mother.

Feruccio gives his details to the monk, who takes the group on a guided tour.

The tour over, the two boys accompany Feruccio's father part of the way back down the lane. 'Goodbye,' says Ennio, shaking the man's hand. 'Bye *papa*,' says Feruccio, kissing his father on both cheeks.

'Write to me as often as you can, you hear?' says the father.

'I'll write every fortnight,' the son promises.

Back in school, Ennio explains the rules and regulations. 'Here, part of the building is a church, and you have to go or they will start saying you're not a Christian,' he says. 'They say that one day when the Communists come you will have to decide who you are. Communists are not Christians but they live just the same and they never die.'

It's easy to feed young boys nonsense, but Feruccio is wise beyond his years. 'Everywhere there are priests and nuns and monks and it's always the same story,' Feruccio says. 'You can't argue with them while you are a boy, but when you're a grown-up and you don't owe anything to anyone, you can do and think what you want.' He continues: 'For the moment you have to study as much as you can and do what they say.'

'Unfortunately that's true. But let's talk about something else,' is Ennio's learned response.

The two become inseparable. They eat together on the huge oak table and wander reluctantly off to church arm-in-arm in the evening after class. If they aren't being collectively punished for misbehaving they spend break periods together too, and that is how Feruccio soon finds out mother hasn't come to visit.

'I'm hungry,' he says one break-time. 'I'm going to get something from my stash.'

'Go ahead,' says Ennio. Feruccio goes off in search of his suitcase, coming back with a sausage and biscuits his mother had left the weekend before.

'Aren't you hungry?' he asks.

'I've got nothing to eat because mamma didn't come,' Ennio says.

'Well eat with me then.' Feruccio offers Ennio a crudely made sandwich.

A minute later: 'Why didn't your mother come?'

'She's afraid that if she does, I'll escape again and I won't come back to school.' It's not a rational explanation, but Ennio can think of no other.

'Can't you tell her that you promise not to escape again and that you like it here?' Feruccio asks. 'Or else what are you going to do at break times if you haven't got anything to eat? Everyone else will be eating what their mothers brought them and you will be left there just watching because you haven't got anything.'

Ennio explains that he has already learnt to live with this problem. 'Sometimes I go out for a wander so that I don't have to stay and watch everybody eating,' he admits. 'And I only come back when I know that everyone has finished. Other times I just say I'm not hungry so that they don't bother me. I can't stay around and have them say things that fuck me off because they're bigger than me and if I get into a fight I'm going to get kicked in.'

'Well, you do as I say,' says Feruccio. 'Write to your mum and tell her what I told you and you'll see she'll be here in no time.'

Ennio says nothing because he has tried writing several times, and hasn't had any letters in return. He is so fed up with the lack of a reply that he has stopped writing completely and has no idea by this time what is happening back in his village. He considers escaping again but thinks better of it.

If mother doesn't write, he thinks, it means she doesn't want to see him.

This conclusion doesn't stop him searching for an explanation, however. In his mind he rolls the problem over time and time again until it starts driving him mad.

After a few months, consolation from Feruccio isn't enough any more. Why doesn't she come? Why hasn't she written?

Again he thinks of escaping and again he decides against it. After a few more days flirting with insanity, he decides not to think about home any more. 'If she wants to see me, she knows where to find me,' he thinks. 'And if she doesn't, well, it's better I forget about her.' Why go home if you're not welcome?

This train of thought brings about a fundamental change. Until the age of twelve, mother has been a little absent but in general life has been sweet. Ennio's concerns are mainly those of a normal kid. But when, on the cusp of adolescence, he is forced to forget about his mother and go about life as if he truly is an orphan, dark thoughts gather.

It is undeniable, he decides. Mother doesn't want to have anything to do with me anymore. I am alone.

This in itself might seem bad, but her abandonment immediately has consequences that are not simply emotional.

She has stopped sending money too, which means Ennio can no longer attend classes. Books for secondary school pupils are costly, and he doesn't have a bean. Nobody actually tells him he can't go to class, but when the yearly enrolment comes around, his name is left off the list. He checks. 'Why haven't your fees been paid?' asks a monk. 'Because my mother hasn't sent any money,' he says. And that is that. What is he to do?

He thinks about leaving school and going to an institute where they teach children a trade, but someone tells him you need money there, too.

So from then on, in the morning, he and one or two other boys in the same penniless position get up with everyone else, watch the others get ready to go to school, go with them from the dorms into the square outside and then watch them walk off to class.

'What the hell am I doing here, watching everyone wander off looking happy?' Ennio thinks. This morning ritual depresses him deeply. He sits around in the monastery alone for hours without seeing anyone. When a monk comes into sight he hides behind a bush or a wall because he doesn't want anybody to see him cry. All he can think is: How am I going to get myself out of this mess? How can I carry on with my studies?

But there is no obvious way out. He can see no option but to stay there and do nothing. When he sees the other kids coming back from school, he takes to avoiding them so that they won't ask, 'Hi, what have you been doing?' He is too ashamed to answer their questions.

Feruccio, as always, is a star. He comes back from school and sets about looking for Ennio straight away. He knows all Ennio's hiding places and after finding him he always asks, 'What do you think you are doing?' No answer is necessary.

'In life, you have to have faith,' says Feruccio. 'You can't let yourself get down about these things.'

'You're right,' says Ennio. 'But how can I find a way out of this mess when nobody wants to help me?'

Feruccio drags Ennio onto the school playground, their little society, where Ennio doesn't leave his side. He doesn't have a lira to his name.

This goes on for a couple more months. Ennio reaches the end of his tether. Wracking his brain for any kind of desperate solution, an idea comes to him; steal enough money for bus fare and go home, go away, go anywhere.

His target is obvious: the church. He knows where the collection box is kept in the chapel of San Giovanni. It's risky, because discovery means expulsion and possibly the *casa di correzione* they have been threatening him with for so long. The chances of getting found out are all the higher given the three separate entrances from which worshippers can surprise a thief. He decides to give it a go all the same.

On the first reconnoitre he discovers the box is locked, so goes rummaging around in the room for a key. He finds one under a coat and slips it into the lock but it won't quite turn, it's too big. It needs filing down, which is what Ennio does back in the dorm the following afternoon with the aid of a file stolen from the head monk's woodwork room.

He has chosen the San Giovanni chapel because it's famous (there are another two less famous chapels). Americans and rich Italians go there to be ripped off by the monks. He has heard they leave stacks of cash, and the rumours turn out to be true. On his second visit, after ensuring no-one is around, he slips the key in nicely and the box opens. Suddenly, he is loaded.

He crams the notes into his pockets as quickly as possible without counting them. His only thought is to get out without getting caught. He will count them later when he finds a quiet spot, he thinks, locking the box.

His haste is just as well. No sooner has he turned around than an old woman comes into the chapel to pray. Like an expert thief, Ennio doesn't take fright. He grabs a duster and pretends he is there to clean. The woman doesn't suspect a thing.

In the courtyard, on a bench, he soaks up the sun for about ten minutes, like a lizard. He then looks up at the windows to see whether anyone is watching. Nobody is, but he decides all the same to find a more secluded spot to count his wad.

He walks out of the college and down the lane before turning uphill towards the olive grove tended by the monks. Ten minutes later he comes to a mound, looks around to make sure there are no monks in sight, and sits.

Counting, he soon gets to three thousand lire; a great haul for a twelve-year-old in 1952. The loot is all in notes of one hundred, fifty, and ten lire.

He divides them up, planning to go down to the village later to change them for smaller denominations. But a new problem surfaces. How is he going to hide the fact he has suddenly become cash-rich? If he tells anyone the word will soon spread and before long some monk will be wanting to know how he has come by all those banknotes. Some jealous individual might even spill the beans.

The best thing, he concludes, is to hide the stash somewhere and spend it slowly, bit by bit, and this is what he does. He wraps the notes, it's quite a bundle, in a sheet of newspaper, and stuffs them into his suitcase.

He gives himself two hundred lire as pocket money but, given that everyone knows he is broke, he is reluctant even to spend this. Perhaps, he thinks, he should give the money to Feruccio, and get him to go into town to buy sweets? In the end he decides to risk it.

Within fifteen minutes he has a big bag of humbugs and a pack of cigarettes.

On his triumphant way back to the college he bumps into two boys he knows. He asks why they aren't in class.

'We've been made to do the cleaning,' one of them says.

'That's horrible, why did they make you do that?' Ennio asks.

'Our parents don't pay our school fees any more, so we have to clean to earn our keep. They're bastards. You'll see, they'll make you do it too.'

Cleaning; what a horrible thought. 'I hate cleaning. If they tell me to clean I'll tell them where to go,' Ennio says confidently. 'In any case, it's better not to think about it. Here, have a humbug.'

He has money, but it is not enough to pay his school fees, which are more than half a year in arrears. And despite having enough for a bus fare, he decides he can't face another trip home followed by another rejection and a humiliating return under escort.

The future looks bleaker than ever. If his debts are not settled he can see himself spending years at school doing nothing. He fears growing up to discover it is too late to do anything about his lack of education.

It's best not to think about it. He asks the other poor boys if they want to play. They agree. They kick a ball around the playground.

The two boys have been cleaning for a while. You can see how unhappy they are from their faces. If he ends up like them he will kill himself, Ennio thinks. The dark thoughts come often now. By playing football he can banish them, but only for a few hours at a time.

For a few more weeks he attempts to keep up with missed schoolwork, and here of course Feruccio is as always his faithful ally. In the evening he patiently explains what has been taught that day, and while he is doing his homework Ennio goes over the exercises himself on a loose sheet of paper. Feruccio is an able teacher, and Ennio is proud that, at least initially, he can keep up without undue effort.

'You never make any mistakes,' says Feruccio one night, 'though you're a bit lazy. You'll never change, Ennio.'

Such a good friend.

Ennio curses his luck when Feruccio has to move away with his family, to Naples, later that year.

'What do you think of my mother?' Ennio asks him shortly before he leaves. It is a direct question. There is no reason to beat about the bush given that he has spent the last two school holidays in Capestrano sitting on his hands. 'I think she has left me,' he says, but Feruccio keeps saying it's simply not possible.

'What could have possessed her to act this way?' Ennio asks.

'Maybe there is a reason you cannot know. There are many reasons that prevent someone from doing what he wants. But one thing I can tell you for sure is your mother has not abandoned you.' His words reassure Ennio as they always do. At the same time, he suspects the truth will out before long.

He sometimes succeeds in deliberately forgetting his mother, in dismissing the subject. If she wants to see him, she will come, though the frequency with which he repeats the same sentence tells its own story.

Alone last thing at night the pain comes flooding back. How could she do this to me? To hurt me? He can't get it out of his head. Some nights, when no answer comes, he just sits there in bed staring at the wall.

Often he cannot help bursting into tears. Attempts to hold it in fail miserably. And in the packed dormitory floods of tears do not go unnoticed. If you drop a pen it makes so much noise everyone hears, so as soon as Ennio starts sobbing all the boys sit up and turn around to see what's going on. He buries his face in the pillow and covers his head with his hands, ashamed.

'What's wrong with him?' some of the boys ask. Feruccio gets out of bed and comes over to his side, cooing calming words.

But by now his admirable attempts to console only make things worse. 'You say you're my friend, so why are you trying to make me stop crying with explanations that have no meaning?' Ennio asks.

He bursts out to the other boys: 'You're all happy because once a month or even once a week you receive a letter from your mothers and you're all safe and sound. You study and you're happy because your mothers send you news and you don't worry about things going wrong because your family will always support you. I, on the other hand, haven't studied all year because my mother hasn't sent me money to buy books and hasn't paid the school, and I don't know how long all this is going to last. I might be here for a long time and no-one will worry about me and when I get older I will come to no good through lack of affection, lack of qualifications, lack of everything everyone else has got. I'll be a loser without parents and my life will be continuous torment.'

Feruccio takes Ennio out into the corridor. 'Listen Ennio, you have to trust me,' he says. 'You have to promise me that this won't happen again because if your mother doesn't contact you we will find another way out of this that's best for you. But you mustn't cry.'

'I will be ruined by this for the rest of my life,' Ennio predicts. 'If my mother doesn't get in contact I'll be here until I'm eighteen or nineteen and I'll leave without qualifications. Without affection from my mother and without a father I'll be ruined. Then when I leave here, what am I supposed to do? If this goes on for a few years it will be too late for me to do anything.'

'We'll write to your mother and ask her what she thinks of you,' Feruccio suggests.

'There's not much point, I've been writing for months,' Ennio says. 'The worst time for me is in the morning when I get up with you lot and have to watch you all go off to class. I too would really like to be in your shoes, to study with you, because I also have ambitions, projects of my own.

'I want to be able to struggle to achieve something, but I feel like everything is screwed up. All the exits are blocked for me. All the doors are closed.

'All hope is gone and I feel that one day my mind will not be strong enough to think any more because of the continual torment of thinking day after day about the same thing. And the worst is that when you see others succeed, you hurt yourself even more, especially as you know that given the chance you could do better than they can.

'It makes me feel so bad. I don't want to see all these things happen. I don't want to open my eyes. So it's only normal that I cry, and crying lets it all out. And then you relax a little and things go smoothly until it happens again. Crying is almost a relief for me, it makes me feel better.'

His speech over, he thanks his friend for listening. 'If you have a lot of homework, be sure to ask me, as I'll help you out,' Ennio says.

'That's all right. I haven't got much,' Feruccio replies.

'You're just saying that because you don't want me to help you,' says Ennio, at which they both laugh.

He carries on as best he can, immersing himself in football. But there is little else to do other than help Feruccio with his homework, working on bits of scrap paper. Reading, for example, is out of the question because the books simply cost too much. The other boys all take their books to school and will lend Ennio theirs only for a few minutes in the evening.

More time passes and he becomes convinced he has become stupid and ignorant. When I was young I was a bright, promising pupil, he tells himself. But it has all come to nothing.

He can't answer the homework questions any more. His school friends make things worse. Fully aware of his predicament, they deliberately ask difficult history questions, calling him a donkey when he can't answer. Shamed once again, he cries. At thirteen he has the education of an eleven-year-old. His torment never stops. Life just keeps spiralling downwards.

After another eight months of laziness and boredom the monks start forcing Ennio to clean. This means sweeping the bedrooms, sponging down the bathrooms and dusting. Two months into this new life and he is sick of it. A reluctant cleaner, he does it badly.

The school director comes back from taking the other children into town, wanting to see what Ennio has accomplished. He enters the dorms and comes out shrieking: 'Where is that good-for-nothing Ennio?'

He is nowhere to be seen of course, and when several hours later the director finally catches up with him, Ennio makes it clear he is fed up with the job. But the director has a heart of stone.

'Do it all again from the top,' he barks. 'That way you'll learn to do it properly the first time.' This becomes a daily routine.

A year later, he is still at it and has lost all hope of ever returning to his studies. He stops thinking about his mother.

Perennially penniless, he does a little more thieving on the side. The director is the next target. When asked to clean the director's office, Ennio swipes one of the two boxes of cigarettes lying on the table. The box is too big to hide under his jumper so he throws it out of the window, down to Mario, the kitchen help, who is standing below and who has no idea what has hit him.

Foraging leads to the discovery of the director's keys, the unlocking of his trunk, and a wad of cash. Ennio takes around two thousand lire, another considerable sum.

No sooner is the money pocketed than he hears footsteps in the corridor. He quickly grabs the bucket and mop and pretends to have been working. The director enters, has a quick look around and says: 'Excellent job. Would you like some chocolate?' Taking the keys from where Ennio has replaced them, the director re-opens the trunk and hands over two of four bars which would have been stolen too if they had not been out of sight under some paperwork.

'There. Is that enough?' he says.

'That will be fine,' Ennio grins. What a result; two thousand lire, cigarettes and chocolate, presents from the victim of the crime.

This is a good day in an otherwise dull, uneventful period.

Many times Ennio goes back to rob the director over the next two years without ever being found out. He always takes enough money for sweets and cigarettes plus a bit more (let's face it, he doesn't need much). If anyone asks how he has come by the money, he says rich Americans have been to the monastery and have given him a tip for showing them around.

It's a good excuse, as there are indeed Americans coming all the time to pray to San Giovanni. Many are actually Italians who moved abroad to work years before and have come back calling themselves Americans.

Success emboldens the thief. Ennio decides to rob the monastery's food store. He has been there many times on errands for the director or for Mario (who is in the kitchen because his parents have abandoned him too).

Over several weeks Ennio makes copies of all the necessary keys, and while the monks are feasting and the kids are at school, he enters the store and takes cigarettes, a bottle of liquor and more chocolates. It is initially designed as an even bigger raid; Ennio has gone as far as interviewing likely candidates for a gang of three. But rather than be bothered with coordinating minions he decides, spontaneously, to do it alone.

Another success, but Ennio is initially concerned his would-be fellow thieves will get annoyed when they find out he has gone solo. There is however little they can do. The profits are not large enough to split among four.

What a pleasure it is in those post-heist days, watching children who have despised him, those who have called him a donkey, come up as nice as pie to ask for a smoke. 'Fuck off,' is the answer they get. It feels good, very good. For a brief period Ennio is back up there at the top of his castle, the *capo dei capi*. He gets cocky again, it's been a while.

The boys in the makeshift gang are keener than ever to get in on the action when they discover how easy it is. So one afternoon, during lunch, they go together with an empty suitcase and fill it with food and more liquor. They take the spoils to a secluded spot near the monastery gardens to eat and drink at their leisure. Not used to the booze, they get so drunk they have to lie down and sleep it off. It's a day to remember.

When the warehouse raid takes place, Ennio's mother hasn't given sign of life for two and a half years. She has been replaced in his life by self-gratification; stealing, smoking, chocolate, and, increasingly, alcohol.

And what of God? The monks can hardly say a word without mentioning God or Christ and in Ennio's eyes are risible creatures.

When he splits his arm open falling from a tree (while stealing nuts) a monk gives him a speech on how God is punishing him for stealing. Ennio asks the monk: 'Couldn't God just have made me fall from the tree without splitting my arm too?'

The wound, a cut right down to the bone, will not heal and the arm swells up massively, so another monk takes Ennio into the village to see the doctor. 'The Lord be praised,' the monk sings out like an idiot when the doctor finally opens the door.

‘I’ll sing your praises if you fix my arm,’ Ennio tells the doctor.

There is no point trusting in God, Ennio decides. You’re better off trusting the individuals you come across, as it is they who are actually going to make a difference to your life. Divine providence? You have to make your own providence, that’s what he says. Those who live in hope most often die that way too.

*

The boys and the girl had gone. The pain was worse and was everywhere. His swollen eye was now shut tight and a continuous high-pitched ring plagued one ear. His mouth was throbbing. It filled with blood as fast as he could spit it out. Working down from head to toe, he thought he may have a dislocated shoulder. Ribs? Was that one broken? He couldn’t tell, but it was as sore as hell.

They’d kicked him in the balls too. It felt as if one testicle had receded into his stomach. This pain alone was enough to keep him doubled over. And then there was the backside. He couldn’t sit on it now; it was too sensitive. It itched constantly.

Hunger. Thirst. Nausea. Ennio retched but threw up nothing.

He couldn’t take another beating, that was for sure. The pounding in his head was too much. Was his skull cracked? He ran his hand, itself swollen, over his head but found no clues.

What now? A nightmare. A real, waking nightmare with no end in sight. Options? End it. Take control. Find a way out. Escape, and if not, take your life. Could he reach that scythe? If he had a rope, he could lasso it, maybe.

He wondered if they had noticed his disappearance back in the capital. Who would mourn his death? His family? Yes of course, but who else? Did he have any real friends? He was close to some of his colleagues, like Alain Saint-Paul, but they were all friends of circumstance. The war had thrown them together. Which friendships would survive the war? Only one name came to mind: Derek.

Despite the unbearable discomfort, Ennio allowed himself a guffaw. Derek, his best friend and at the same time the biggest idiot he had ever met. His victim.

How could a man so intelligent be ruled by his prick? Derek was so repressed it was easy to manipulate him, to bend his will in any direction. Was Ennio ever that naive? He wondered, unsure.

*

That summer, for the first time, he sees two boys in bed together. The three of them have been put in one dormitory (one is from Venice and another from the Abruzzo near to where Ennio was born).

He enters and sees them there, as naked as the day they were born. One is on the bed with his backside in the air. Standing behind him is the other with his cock hard, excited. He is putting it wherever he pleases. Ennio's entrance doesn't seem to bother them. They just carry on, at one point changing positions.

When they have finished one kisses the other and thanks him. He then gets dressed and walks out, smiling and winking to a dumbfounded Ennio.

Approaching the boy (the one from Venice) left sprawled on the bed, Ennio asks for an explanation.

The boy laughs and replies: 'You can see you're no expert in the ways of the world.'

'Please talk sense,' Ennio pleads.

The thirteen-year-old continues: 'When I am in Venice I go with women, but this year I haven't been home because I met him.' He points in the direction of the departed boy. 'I invited him home but he wanted to stay here, so I've stayed here with him, because he gives me pleasure.'

'Does your mother know about this?'

'My mother lost her husband years ago, but she is still a beautiful woman. I've seen her in bed with other women. They were kissing each other and wrapping their bodies around each other like snakes. When they stopped I went over to the bed with a hard-on but they wouldn't let me do anything. They just stayed there without moving.'

It's an odd world, Ennio reckons.

According to the Venetian's story, after a few more silent rejections he goes to his mother's bed and actually asks her for sex. 'Why don't you go and chat up a woman yourself?' the depraved mother replies.

'Because I'm afraid,' the boy says. 'I'd prefer it with you because I know you.'

'If you're afraid of women, why don't you find yourself a boyfriend?' she says. 'When you find one, stay with him if he gives you pleasure, or if not find another, and then another, until you get used to it. It's possible that with women you will be unhappy, like I was with your father, but maybe with a boy you'll feel more comfortable.'

A truly mind-blowing conversation for Ennio's ears. He is literally left speechless. It takes him a while to formulate another question: 'Do you think you will keep seeing that boy?'

'For the moment I have to put up with him, but when I have found another one it will be different,' the kid answers. He shares the money his mother sends with his boyfriend.

'Well don't get me involved because I hate all that stuff,' Ennio tells him. 'I hope you will have a long rosy life together.' It's all too weird. Ennio decides he wants them out of the room.

The Venetian makes for the door, but before closing it behind him, he turns and says: 'Look Ennio, in a few days my mother is coming to visit me, maybe you would like to get to know her?'

'It would be an honour.'

Alone again, Ennio lies down on the bed, the conversation spinning around in his mind. A new world has opened up; an odd, perverted world he never thought existed. The sordid sexual act makes him sick, but he finds it fetching that the boys are so attached to each other. What strikes him more than anything else is their adult nature. A thirteen-year-old with the mind of a man of thirty or forty. The comments alluding to naivety also strike a cord. What kind of woman could have raised this child-man?

The day of the woman's arrival comes quickly. The son prepares for the rendezvous by dressing up in his best clothes and greasing his hair. When the taxi pulls up he rushes down the stairs, throwing his arms around her and giving her a kiss. The boyfriend is there too. The mother kisses them both, as if blessing their union. Ennio watches from behind the bay windows until he is called out for an official introduction. He has to go outside because women are not allowed in the monastery.

'This is Ennio,' says the son.

Ennio looks her straight in the eyes, not to confront her but to delve into her soul. She shakes his hand, gives him a smile and says to the boys: 'Let's all go for a walk, shall we?'

He accompanies them a short distance but then changes his mind, says he has homework to do, and peels off from the group. He returns to his original position behind the bay windows in order to watch this beautiful woman disappear into the woods with her son and his male lover.

It is difficult from the way she holds herself to imagine her depraved nature. But from the shape of her face you can see that she is not the kind of woman who leads a normal life. She is too beautiful to take life seriously. She loves life, it is clear. Perhaps her vice is more apparent in her body movements. She smokes, after all.

He thinks about her long curly blonde hair, dropping over her forehead and falling onto her shoulders. Her eyes are so expressive they are prisms through which you can read her mind. She has thick red lips, a nice chest and a tight skirt that hides little. A well constructed woman.

Thinking about her gives Ennio a hard-on, so he goes to the bathroom to relieve himself. His imagined sex with her is however spoilt a little by the knowledge that she prefers women. What a shame that is.

Before the trio disappears into the woods Ennio notices the son introduce his mother to a passing monk. Instead of looking at her as Ennio does, the monk keeps his eyes fixed firmly on the ground as if he has never seen a woman before and does not want to risk temptation. The monks want to give the impression they do not go with women because God does not desire it. So the conversation is over pretty quickly. The monk leaves without offering his hand. Ennio can see him mouth 'Jesus Christ be praised' as he walks away. Ennio can't help thinking it is the blonde who deserves praise, not Him.

Shortly after Ennio becomes conscious of someone having entered the adjoining room. Curious, he looks through the keyhole and much to his disgust sees the same monk, on his own, lying on a couch with his trousers down, enjoying the woman from a distance as if he were a dog; a nauseating scene that makes Ennio want to flee the monastery. He goes back out to look for the visitors, aiming to distract himself in conversation. But after only a few steps he stops, as he can't resist looking back at the monastery window. And sure enough he sees the monk, back on his feet and stretching as if he had had a little snooze, a little red in the face and smiling. Their eyes meet and the monk seems to react to the mocking intensity of Ennio's glare. Until a few minutes ago he looked sad, but now it looks as if he's enjoying life again, Ennio reckons.

He changes his mind again, goes back inside, drawn by God-knows-what to seek out the fat little man and talk to him. In the hallway he spies him walking down the stairs.

'Nice day!' Ennio says.

'Beautiful day, if a little hot!' the monk replies.

'A glass of wine would go down a treat, wouldn't it?'

'You fancy some?' the monk says out of the blue.

And just like that, the two trot down to the cellar for two glasses of wine and polite conversation.

Ennio has developed a theory about monks. They are good people, mostly. They look miserable because they are lonely and have to take orders from old, even more miserable, people who get no enjoyment out of life any more. They also have to live inside the same walls for many years at a time, their only distraction being the odd nun every now and again. And having a roll with a nun cannot happen that often. Most monks would give all they have just for a bit of happiness.

The Venetian's fantastic mother stays for lunch (she has to eat in a different building) and then invites the boys to accompany her back to the station as she has to leave. Ennio says he is tired, that his arm is hurting. He is too lazy to go down into the village. He watches her walk down the path, admiring her arse. Maybe, one day when he is older, he'll have a woman with an arse like that, he thinks, lying in the grass, whiling the rest of the day away.

Within weeks, he does in fact have a girl of his own; the daughter of a woman who works in the convent in the neighbouring village. He has seen her around.

'Do you want to come for a walk in the forest with me?' he asks her. The answer is yes. Ennio is about to lift her down from the windowsill on which she is sitting when a monk walks by.

In the courtyard, in the heat and the dark, he imagines her face coming towards him with the breeze.

He sees her once more, two days later. As always, he is on his way to the valley for a morning walk. Passing in front of the convent she is there, on the steps, waiting for him.

'Where are you going?' she asks.

'For a walk in the woods, do you want to come?'

He gets her moving quickly because he doesn't want anyone seeing them together. Nobody minds their own business in the countryside. When under cover of the trees she seems happy enough.

'I've been waiting for you to pass by,' she says. 'Do you want to play the game we played last time?'

But Ennio is worried about hurting her and uncertain about touching her. He undresses her, takes her bra and underwear off, but this time only puts it between her legs, not inside her. Again, he wipes her clean with a handkerchief.

'Do you like what I do to you?' he asks.

A one-word answer: Yes.

'Remember to say nothing to your mother.' She promises. He drops her off at the convent and spends the rest of the morning lying on his back under a tree.

*

The pain wasn't just physical, he discovered. Mentally too he felt himself slipping.

Caravadossi's aria had become deformed and taken on a piercing metallic sound. He couldn't get it out of his head. At unexpected times it would warp again into a deep, throbbing noise, the notes dancing around on the lining of his skull. He wished it would stop.

There were also signs he was beginning to hallucinate. He dreamed, awake or asleep he couldn't tell, that he had broken his chains and climbed up the farm tools decorating the walls of the barn to the roof, where he punched a hole and climbed out before flying away like a bird.

As soon as he snapped out of this reverie, it began again, more believable this time. And then again.

Physically speaking, thirst was once again the main concern. He had been given water only once, and his parched mouth was ready to suck on anything; the wood of the yoke, his own blood.

And then there was boredom, equally painful. Just sitting there waiting for his fate to be decided, not knowing whether he would be there for a day or a lifetime. Nothing to do but count strands of straw.

Despite the possibility of another beating, he was almost happy when the barn door opened.

The old wizened man was back with another four men of similar age. As they walked purposefully towards Ennio, a little figure darted out from among the assembled legs. It was the girl, carrying two bowls. She placed them just in front of him and stood there, looking into his eyes for just an instant, before scampering off.

They contained water and rice. Ennio's snout dropped greedily.

A minute later, when he rose for air, the old man approached with his hand outstretched. Ennio at first feared a new slap, but the movements were gentle and trustworthy.

The old man wanted to inspect his wounds, it transpired. He then conversed with his companions, who were in all probability village elders. Ennio's best guess was that they did not approve of what they saw. Perhaps the beatings had taken place without their knowledge.

More conversation followed, and Ennio's passport was handed around. After five minutes, they left without addressing him.

Thirst quenched, boredom returned.

He had to keep his mind engaged. He had to play games in his head. He thought of testing his vocabulary. How do you say 'beating' in French? And in English?

What was the best meal he had ever eaten? Was it the *lasagne* in that village outside Rome? Or the *polenta* his mother used to make?

He decided to review every year, from January to December, with a view to deciding when he had been happiest. Had the war made him truly happy? Vietnam had given him his pride, no mean thing. He had arrived in Saigon a coward but could now look in the mirror and see a real man. For the first time too he was not afraid to say what he did for a living. But hadn't he been happier living in Paris? There was a time there when he had both Derek's support and the freedom to play the field, the ideal situation. Or Brussels? Yes, he was happy there too with Gordon and Peggy, though it was only a short stay.

And what about the most miserable year of his life to date? Well, that was easy...

*

The boys are rushing around getting ready for the start of term, talking about the books they have bought, how much they cost, which ones are the most expensive. Ennio listens and says nothing. All he wants to know is how he will end up. Over the summer the school director says he will try to help out, to find a way for Ennio to keep studying, but there is no follow-up. A few days into the new term there is still no news. Ennio resigns himself to another year without schooling. Perhaps, he begins to think, he will never again hold a pen between thumb and forefinger.

The old routine resumes. In the morning he sees the school boys line up in front of the monastery three-by-three, like little soldiers, wearing new shoes and with gel in their short-cropped hair, waiting to wander down to the village for their lessons. Every morning he watches them go, murmuring the latest gossip, disappearing down the lane.

'Have you been told to start cleaning yet?' Ennio asks another penniless boy.

'Not yet,' the boy replies with a smile. 'Maybe the director is letting us rest for the first few days.'

It in fact takes the director a couple of months before he gets sick of seeing Ennio hanging around. Instructions arrive: Start cleaning again. Ennio feels obliged to acquiesce.

When in the forest with a virgin girl he is in his element, but in polite educated company he is a donkey; a boy who has no choice but to obey.

After a few days cleaning, it is announced that a kitchen help is required. Mario has left. The director thinks immediately of Ennio. 'You have to earn your keep in the kitchen,' he says. Ennio complies, though he loathes the idea of being stuck among the pots and pans all day.

'I hate the kitchen but given I don't study and I don't earn my keep, I guess I should work,' Ennio tells him. For a moment he thinks he sees compassion in the director's eyes.

He is introduced to the cook and told to peel potatoes. The cook has his hair tied back and a large, tidy moustache that must take a while to put straight every morning. He also has a huge stomach like most cooks and can't be more then one-metre-forty tall. Ennio towers over him. Every now and again he lets out a lyrical note. 'I've been put to work with Caruso,' Ennio marvels.

Three hours later he is told to stop peeling. He has been at it for so long he thinks he has been forgotten. Knowing that there is surely more work to do, Ennio sits and says nothing. If he asks, he will be given a new task straight away, he is sure.

'What, are you already tired?' the cook asks, looking at him.

'Well, as you hadn't given me anything else to do I thought I would wait until you did.'

'Don't worry, there is always work to be done in the kitchen. You can start by washing the pots and pans.'

It is disgusting. Ennio has never put his hands in greasy water before. They are soon covered in filth. This time, when he finishes, he tells the cook he has to spend a penny and goes out into the courtyard for a rest, some fresh air and a cigarette. The thought of going back inside is depressing so he stays outside. Within a few minutes a monk comes out. 'The cook is looking for you,' he says.

'I've only been in there for half a day and already they can't do without me,' Ennio tells him.

The cook is clearly annoyed. 'Where have you been?' he says, three times with increasing volume. Ennio invents a story about having to run an errand for the head of security, a canny trick given the cook and the head of security don't get along. The cook forgets momentarily about Ennio and concentrates on his food, mumbling obscenities about his enemy.

It's soon midday and the monks arrive for lunch, followed by the students half an hour later. For the rush hour another kitchen help arrives, a boy called Andrea whom Ennio does not know.

'Given that he is here, can I go now?' Ennio asks. They both give him a dirty look.

'We need two of you in the kitchen. Mario has left, so that's why you've been brought in,' says the cook. Ennio sits in the corner and lets the other boy get on with it as he seems to know what he is doing. This earns him just a few moments of respite.

'Come over here so that you can learn quickly,' says the cook. 'It's in your own interest because you can earn a load of money from this business and it's a safe trade too.' Ennio pretends to take notice. Learning is after all a way of getting by without actually doing any work. He doesn't care a bit for the catering trade. There is no way he is going to end up doing boring work for a living.

After lunch he wolfs down some food himself. This is the only advantage of working in a kitchen; you can eat as much as you want. He then slips out for a nice long walk.

When he returns, at 6pm, the cook is already looking for him. 'Where have you been?'

'I thought the kitchen didn't open again until late so I went for a walk,' Ennio says, quite truthfully.

'But didn't you know that you have to go with Andrea and feed the pigs?'

Ennio works until ten o'clock that night. When he is dismissed he is told to be back at six the next morning. Instead of going to his dorm he goes up onto the roof to smoke a cigarette.

Look what it has come to. They won't let you study, they make you work in the kitchen from dawn till dusk without pay, and now you have to feed the pigs. How long will this last? Isn't there a way out of this horrible job?

Things deteriorate further the next day when he discovers that in addition to preparing milk for the other students he has to help out with the early morning mass. Here too he avoids work, initially, on the grounds that he has no knowledge of church procedure; if he isn't robbing the collection box, the inside of a church is the last place he wants to be. But this is only ever going to be a short-term solution. He is given a book on ecclesiastic rituals and three weeks to learn its contents. From a pew he watches the priest's movements so as to be able to shadow him properly.

Months pass and Ennio learns all the required techniques, from feeding pigs to washing saucepans and singing hymns. Andrea, a decent boy, is now the only friend he has; there is no time to hang around with anyone else. When the cook isn't looking the two boys steal food and drink and sometimes smoke the cook's cigars. They have mock fights with each other, splashing soapy water all over the kitchen and then rushing around to clean it up. If they are feeling particularly mischievous the cheese and the milk fly around the kitchen too. When the cook leaves the room they smear the floor near the door with grease in an attempt to trip him up on his return.

Their friendship makes the work bearable, and they come to rely on each other. They tell each other everything. Any problem, even Ennio's mother issue, is thrashed out over a meal, with neither boy getting up until it is solved to someone's satisfaction.

But one day, for no apparent reason, Andrea does not turn up. The cook claims he has simply decided to go back to his village on a whim. Not trusting the cook's explanation, Ennio suspects Andrea must have been kicked out. He can't accept that his friend, his first real friend since Feruccio, has just disappeared. He asks the cook for Andrea's address. The cook hands it over and then immediately seems to regret having done so. He starts mumbling that he isn't sure, that he has probably taken it down wrongly.

Ennio suspects the truth is being hidden from him. 'It doesn't matter, I'll try to write to him all the same. It's worth spending thirty lire on a stamp when it's for someone you care about.'

The cook is about to reply to this, but stops himself. He doesn't have the courage to give Ennio a proper explanation, and so just stands there with his mouth half open. He tries to change the subject but Ennio doesn't pay any attention. Tired of talking to himself, the cook just shuts up.

Ennio goes out to feed the pigs, pausing to lean up against an outside wall and smoke a cigarette Andrea has given him just the day before. He shivers at the thought that Andrea has simply left without saying goodbye. Had he done something to offend him? He can't think of anything.

Melancholy overcomes him as he recalls the many days Andrea helped chase away his sadness.

Andrea's disappearance is a new low point. It triggers a dark depression. Tears come in one big burst. Sitting in the stables, staring at the wall, listening to the pigs eat around him, Ennio breaks down. Was he destined to live a life of loneliness, unloved and friendless?

There are footsteps outside. A priest calls his name. 'Why are you looking so down?' he asks, finding the red-eyed boy. There is no answer, so he repeats the question in different words: 'What's wrong with you?'

Something snaps. Ennio jumps up and shouts: 'What's wrong with me? I've done nothing wrong! What do you think I've done?'

A pause and a snarl: 'In any case, I don't have to tell you. These are my own, personal, things and I will keep them to myself.'

Another pause. The hysterical fit subsides.

'I apologise,' Ennio tells the monk. 'I just want to be alone with my problems, and I was hoping that no-one would see me. If you were in my shoes, you would not feel too good either.'

'What happened doesn't matter,' the monk says. 'I am sure that if you confide in me you will find that I can help you.'

'It's not that anything special has happened to me, it's just that I feel like dying,' says Ennio, grabbing his buckets and rushing back to the kitchen.

The cook's face looks ugly enough to slap. For the rest of the day Ennio peels potatoes without giving his boss the time of day, without addressing him once. He just does his job and goes off to bed at the end of the day. He does however say goodnight on the way out as he knows it is disrespectful to leave the presence of an older person without saying anything. The cook makes a special effort to say 'goodnight' very sweetly.

In bed with the light out, the thoughts of his departed friend return. What could possibly have possessed him to leave without saying something? He can't sleep, and gets up, determined to write a letter. He finds pen and paper and writes a short note asking Andrea why he has left so suddenly. He puts a stamp on the letter and sneaks quickly out of college and down into the village to post it.

Nothing comes back. Was it Andrea's correct address?

Once again, truly alone, but this time with no desire to make new friends, Ennio becomes a hermit, a recluse who knows what everyone else is up to but who doesn't want to get involved. He takes long walks in the woods, preferring the trees as company. He takes to sitting under a big oak tree in the shade and just waiting there until it is time to go to work. He no longer laughs or smiles, and walks around with a serious look on his face. He loses touch with the gang, apart from when he needs to barter goods for pocket money. Any spare cash is used to buy books. Ennio's life now revolves around reading. And stealing of course; he continues to take the money he needs from other people.

The work doesn't let up. First it was the kitchen, then feeding the pigs, then changing the pigs' straw three times a week. The next task is taking the turkeys to pasture, and then the sheep too. He ends up working from dawn until past dusk with hardly a break.

He does it with enthusiasm at first because it fills the day, leaving no time for storm clouds to gather in his head. Then it gets embarrassing. When it's time to bring the turkeys back to their pen, Ennio has to cross the square in front of the church. Sometimes he comes across boys from school on their break. They make fun of him; make him feel three inches tall. He goes red as a beetroot with shame. The next time they see him, the insults have been pre-prepared. All he can do is lower his head. He says nothing, but back in the pen, the waterworks recommence. Once they called him 'donkey', now they call him 'turkey boy'. It's more than humiliating.

To guide the turkeys he uses a big stick. 'Hi there, turkey boy!' comes one call from close range. Nerves tingling, Ennio swings the stick around and crashes it into the boy's head. He falls straight to the ground and looks as if he has been knocked right out. Quickly blood begins to gather on the stone slabs beneath his head.

The other boys rush up to help while Ennio moves calmly out of the way. Four of them carry the injured boy off by the arms and legs. They enter a house on the square, shutting the door after them. Those that remain stare at Ennio with fear written large on their faces. Ennio stares back. When he has had enough he simply walks off. The turkeys, fortunately, are already back in their pen. They know the path by heart. He closes the gate behind them.

It isn't long before the college director finds him. 'You must be mad!' he shouts. 'You could have killed him!' Ennio lowers his eyes in an admission of regret. But the director doesn't stop shouting.

Ennio interrupts. 'Do you think it is fair, director, that I, who have agreed to do this job without earning as much as a piece of bread in return, that I have to put up with a load of insults as if I were scum from the local prison? Tell me if you think it's fair?'

The director is flummoxed and pauses to collect his thoughts. 'But he was much smaller than you,' he chimes in eventually.

'But you are the ones who teach them manners and so surely you teach them to respect people who are older than they are? They have been making fun of me for days and I couldn't put up with it any more. I think it happened at the right time, and that I have probably cured them of their vice for good.'

The boys are still young and don't understand all that is at stake, the director says.

'Maybe from now on they will realise that I am dangerous and that it's better if they don't say anything to me,' Ennio declares. Not wanting to admit that the boy is to blame at least in part, the director says nothing more. He leaves, a grimace on his face.

Ennio stares into space, thinking about the day that lies ahead of him; up at six to help the priest during mass; straight into the kitchen to make feed for the pigs; peel potatoes; prepare lunch for students and monks; take the turkeys out; clean the pigsty; back to the kitchen to help prepare dinner; wash the dishes. He's working like a slave, and just because he is studying a few books this little runt of a boy thinks he has the right to insult him. Next time he'll knock him down and make sure he doesn't get back up.

*

Another day, more rice and water. Caravadossi was still there, a ghost haunting Ennio's head.

It was increasingly difficult to keep the spirits up. Depression pressed down on the prisoner like a large, thick, heavy board.

The mind tricks didn't work anymore. The only game that sparked any interest was, 'what will I do if I get out here?' Marry a good woman. That was the first resolution. Derek wouldn't approve, he knew, but that was of no importance. It was time to stop messing around with men. Why should he keep pretending he liked it?

Buy a farm, somewhere quiet and peaceful; that was number two. He needed somewhere to rest and recover.

More tears of self-pity. Quiet ones this time, dropping methodically down his cheeks and blotching what remained of his trousers.

This was no way to die, he thought. He was prepared, as much as one could be, for an exploding grenade, a burst of machinegun fire or a plane crash. A few deep breaths, a silence and then you were gone; this was how he imagined it to be. But left to rot in a barn? This wasn't what fate had in store, surely.

The door creaked open again. The little girl was back, tip-toeing in. What was she after? Did she want to watch him get beaten to a pulp again?

She was carrying something in her hand, he couldn't see what. She started to smile and then to giggle.

'What's the matter with you?' said Ennio. 'You're as mad as I am you little cow.' He couldn't help but smile himself, and wondered for a second if he was not hallucinating. Was she really there?

The girl giggled some more and then scurried past him to an area behind the yoke. He lost sight of her but could hear her rustling around near the floor. She was making the chains clank; she was lifting them and letting them fall. Then there was a click.

She squealed with delight and came back to stand before Ennio, lifting up one hand. A key. A lingering look into Ennio's eyes, a lover's look, and she scampered out of the barn.

Slowly, cautiously, Ennio pulled at his chains. They were loose. He continued to pull, still slowly so as not to make too much noise. They came completely free. The girl had released him. He was still in the barn, but suddenly, a bright light tore through the depression. Was he about to break free?

*

After more than three years without news from his mother, Ennio is an institutionalised slave. He is the school dogsbody. No job is too low or too demeaning.

He thinks and thinks and thinks. How long can this go on? He has missed so much schooling he has no hope of catching up. He has come to terms with his ignorance. So why is he whiling away his days in a kitchen, working for free? But if he left, where would he go? To his mother's house? But is she even alive?

He decides to go and talk to the director, whose parents he knows live only a couple of kilometres from Morrea.

In the director's office, he unloads his spleen. This was not the life he wanted, Ennio declares. He wants to leave this school as soon as possible. Straight away.

'Haven't you heard from your mother at all?' the director asks.

'Almost four years have gone by without a word.'

'So you want to leave, but where are you going to go?' Ennio can tell by his tone that the director wants to help. 'Do you want to become a monk?' he asks.

Without hesitation; no.

'I want to help you, but what can I do?' the director asks.

'You're going home for Christmas? Yes? Good. Please do me just one favour if you could. You live just two kilometres from my village. If it's not too much of a problem would you go there and find out what has happened to my mother? It's a small village and even if she is not there I am sure if you ask around someone will know what's going on. If you could do me this favour I would be very grateful, because at least that way I would know if she is alive or not. If she is, I can go there myself.'

The director answers with kindness. 'As soon as I go on holiday I will find out about your mother, and if she is in the village I will try to talk with her, but don't get your hopes up.'

'It's something I need to know. When you are sure about something, when you know for better or worse, the question doesn't rattle around in your head like a nightmare for the rest of your life.'

The interview over, Ennio leaves the office and returns to slavery. There are still two months to go before Christmas. He counts the days. Sometimes he counts them three or four times just to make sure. Sometimes he miscounts; there are more days left than he thinks. But slowly and surely the calendar rolls away; twenty days left, ten days, one week.

The last week seems eternally long. Ennio tries to work harder in the hope time will pass quicker. And then, with just four days left, panic hits. What if the director comes back with bad news?

On the day of the director's departure, Ennio wants to see him to remind him not to forget the favour, but the director seems to be in such a rush. On the landing, by the front door, the director approaches. Ennio searches for something to say that won't annoy him, but the only thing that comes into his head is: 'Can I carry your bag to the station?'

The offer accepted, the two walk down to the village, Ennio struggling with the suitcase. Ten minutes later and he is again on the verge of reminding the director, but is too nervous to talk.

They arrive at the station and Ennio puts down the load. The director turns to him and says: 'As soon as I get to my village I will try to go to yours and find out about your mother.'

Satisfied, Ennio helps him onto the train and waves him goodbye.

On the way back to the college he is tempted to pray, that's how much he desires good news. But a prayer serves no purpose, he decides. Does it really make any difference if she is dead?

He works doubly hard over the holidays, his nerves frayed raw. The news he is to receive will be decisive. Good or bad, he will be able to start making plans for a life beyond Capestrano.

The day he is told the director is due back, Ennio waits for him outside, sitting on the wall. He begins his vigil early in the morning. Four hours later, the director walks up the path. Ennio's heart begins to beat loudly. Good news? Bad news? Rather than run up, he decides at first to wait sitting on the wall. But within a minute desire gets the better of him. He sprints down the path, both desperately excited and terrified of the unknown.

'How did your trip go?' he asks.

'Well,' says the director. Ennio again offers to carry a bag, ending up with the heavier of the two. It is so heavy he has to keep switching it from one hand to the other.

'Having trouble?' the director asks.

'Not at all. It's light,' Ennio pretends, as there are only fifty metres left to the front door.

'Take it to my room,' the director says as they get inside. 'And then I have to talk to you about your mother.'

That phrase, 'about your mother' makes Ennio's mind whir. Does it mean she is sick? Or dead? Or maybe he hasn't come straight out with the news because everything is fine, and therefore the telling can wait a few more minutes.

He considers getting drunk. If he gets bad news while drunk, he reasons, he can take it with a laugh and a smile. In the case of good news, he can carry on drinking to celebrate. What time was it? Would the monks' cellar be open? Could he nip down for a litre of wine?

A good plan, he decides. He finds the cellar door open and walks through nonchalantly, assured that he has a good excuse – his celebration – if anyone catches him pilfering.

And someone does. No sooner does he find a bottle, unscrew the cap and swig, than two hands grab him from behind.

His excuse on the tip of his tongue, he turns around. And what a sight he sees; a thirty-year-old red-faced, monk, drunk as a skunk, hair dishevelled and tottering dangerously. The sight is so ridiculous, Ennio laughs. 'What do you want?' he says.

The monk says nothing but grabs Ennio tighter still, pushing him towards a dark corner of the cellar. He then pulls up his tunic to reveal an even uglier image: his private parts, at full speed ahead. He attempts to ruck against Ennio's flank.

Giving him a big push, Ennio sends him sprawling to the floor, where he stays for a full minute staring gormlessly at the ground. With a start he then looks up and stares straight into Ennio's eyes.

Afraid of more physical confrontation, Ennio grabs a stick lying nearby. Before the monk can stand he gives him a big whack on the back, and another on the shoulder. This time the monk stays down.

Without worrying about him, Ennio takes the wine and escapes out into the courtyard. To hell with them, he tells himself. These monks are both miserable and queer. He finishes off the bottle while hanging around in the kitchen, killing a couple of hours.

Another boy eventually sobers him up with a few words. 'The director wants to talk to you.'

The judge sits behind his desk.

'I sent for you because I have to talk to you about something very important,' he says. 'It's about your mother.'

Ennio is invited to sit.

'I've been to see her. She's fine.'

A burst of joy. Until these words are spoken, Ennio is convinced she is dead. 'She's coming to see you soon,' the director says.

'But why didn't she come before now?'

'Because she is afraid,' the director replies.

'Afraid of what?'

The director doesn't answer this question. Ennio can see from his face that he too is afraid, afraid to reveal the real reason. Instead, he recounts other details of their meeting and gives Ennio a package from his mother. There is a letter inside which she has dictated to him.

Back in his dorm, Ennio opens the package and finds it is full of sweets. He opens the letter too, but before he can finish reading he breaks down in tears, burying his face in his pillow. He can hardly believe his mother is finally back in touch. She has included a photo of herself, an image he has long since forgotten. She looks young and smiles invitingly. He sees his resemblance.

'How are you, my little one?' she asks. 'It's been so long, I can't wait to see you again!' There is no explanation of her absence.

Ennio takes a sheet of paper and writes back immediately. He tells her how happy he is to receive her package, how happy her letter has made him.

'I can now stop living in a dream-world' he tells her. 'I no longer have to worry something has happened to you. I feared you might even have died. Now that I am sure you are alive I can also look forward to seeing you again. I just want to hug you, mamma!'

That night he dreams he is dancing with angels.

The next day, upon waking, Ennio is transformed. Work suddenly gives him satisfaction. Life is again worth living. Overnight his depression, his unhappiness, have disappeared. Both the monks and the students notice the change.

'What's got into to you?' they ask.

*

Shaking his head at his amazing luck, Ennio made for the barn door. It was night time and he knew he had to make his escape attempt immediately. He wasn't sure how many hours there were until dawn. He thought about arming himself with a farming tool from the barn but decided against it, convinced this would slow him down. He steeled himself to run. The plan was simple; if someone saw him, or as soon as he heard the first shout of alarm, he would run for his life in any direction, preferably into undergrowth. If no-one saw him, he would creep out of the village.

He pissed on the hinges before opening the door, hoping this would prevent any creaking. They creaked a little all the same, but he didn't need to open it far to slip out. Standing made him dizzy. As much as he tried he couldn't ignore the pain in his leg. He was limping, but as the door widened he felt the adrenalin seeping through his veins, awakening his senses. He knew that if forced to sprint his brain would override any other feeling and concentrate on maximising speed.

A full moon bathed the cluster of huts with white warm light. The stars were brilliantly bright, almost dazzling. The night air had a magic quality to it. Ennio sipped it in, so pure.

A quick look around revealed no sign of life, no lights and no noise other than animals grunting from some distance away. He stood there, unsure of his bearings and willing to update the plan. Which direction now? He must find his way back onto the road. Head off in any other direction and he might get lost.

He calculated roughly the required direction and then added a detour that would keep him at a safe distance from village huts he saw. Without further consideration he set off, on all fours at first, creeping, and then half-crouching, half-running as he made progress. After a hundred yards he wished he had closed the barn door behind him, but it was too late to turn back.

He made the road without incident other than cuts to his feet from sharp stones. Like good villagers, they slept soundly until woken by the chickens.

Elated to the extent that he had to stifle yelps, he began jogging along the road in the direction he thought he had come down. His mind turned for the first time in days back to Cambodia and the journalists who would by now be expecting only news of his death. He allowed himself to believe he might see them again, that he might be able to tell of his ordeal.

After around half an hour and by now so weak there was no question of going an inch further, he left the road, dived deep into the undergrowth, lay down and slept on his hands.

At dawn he was woken by the sound of engines. Still exhausted and once again weak with hunger and thirst, he poked his head out from behind a tree and saw a patrol, two jeeps, coming down the road.

Cambodians, he thought; though later, when asked to tell his story to the press pack, he couldn't explain how he knew who they were.

He stepped out into the road and waved them down. When the first soldier approached he held his hands together in a prayer and then pointed to himself. 'Journalist... Italian... Phnom Penh,' he said.

They ushered him into the back and drove away. Inside, soldiers yawned, too tired to speak. They eyed him expressionlessly. Those who were sitting closest gave him more room. Ennio was suddenly aware of his wretched smell. Five kilometres further on the jeep stopped in front of a large old building, a dilapidated mansion. The driver motioned Ennio to dismount. He obeyed. The driver pointed towards the building and patted Ennio on the back. 'Go, go,' he said, before getting back behind the wheel and driving off.

Zombie-like, limping heavily and now shaking violently, Ennio walked up the driveway to the front entrance, above which he saw a large cross and an inscription in Latin. He rang the doorbell and stood there.

After five minutes the door opened slowly and a person in a habit appeared. Great; more nuns. Ennio chuckled. Another bloody convent.

There was no water for a bath but the nuns gave him clothes; a black, torn tunic and baggy trousers he had to hold up with string.

'Tomorrow,' a nun said in French. 'Tomorrow you go to hospital.'

Fed and watered, he fell asleep quickly on a mat in the corner of the entrance hall. As he nodded off he congratulated himself. He'd done it. He'd got out.

*

However much he talks of his desire to return to his village, the monks think it's a bad idea.

'Things are really bad up there,' they say. 'There's not enough work and no-one has any money, they all go around badly dressed.'

After a few days of this useless advice the assistant director calls Ennio into his office, saying he has something 'very serious' to talk about.

'You're a good boy and you haven't had much luck with your family,' he says. 'I want you to think about becoming a monk.'

The tone is so earnest Ennio wants to laugh, but out of respect he holds it in. He explains simply that after years of monastery life he is already fed up. Imagine how he would feel after spending a lifetime in one?

Sensing they are not keen on granting their slave his freedom, Ennio marches straight back to the director and asks to be driven home. The director is also not keen but is pressed to the point he has to agree, provided Ennio waits a few months. 'It's mid-January and we are lucky here because here there is no snow,' the director says. 'But your village is at altitude. They must have a metre of snow at the moment. Wait until spring and I'll take you. In April or May.'

Ennio suspects this is an excuse to keep him working a few more months for free, but he swallows his pride yet again, returning dutifully to the kitchen to scour pots and pans until April, at which point he demands a firm date for his departure.

'May 28,' says the director. Leaving the office, Ennio does a hop, skip and jump.

'Why are you so happy?' the cook asks.

'Because in just a few days, we won't see each other again.'

May 28 finally arrives, and the college director makes good on his promise. As the car approaches Morrea, Ennio's excitement turns to concern. The photo his mother has sent might be old, he thinks. Would he recognise her?

After three hours on the road they arrive at the director's house, just down the road from Ennio's village. They have lunch, after which the director says: 'I don't feel like driving you up the hill to your village. I'm too tired. I'll get you a ride with the postman.'

They leave straight away. As the postman's tiny car takes the hairpin bends upwards, the two glance at each other a few times without saying a word. It is Ennio who breaks the silence.

'How long have you being doing this job?' he asks.

'Four years.'

Ennio asks if he knows his mother.

'Very well,' comes the reply. 'Her name is Giacinta but they call her *la Giacintona*.'

'Why is that?'

'I think it's because she is a little fat, and the name just came automatically.'

The postman looks at Ennio sternly. 'What are you going to do up there? Things are really bad. I wouldn't be seen dead up there.'

'Every now and again you have to go and see your relatives, don't you?'

'That's a good reason,' says the postman, before going on to chat, without any encouragement, about Ennio's sister who, unbeknown to Ennio, has been living in Rome for years.

They have to stop and walk the last few hundred metres because the street paving still hasn't been finished. What ignorant people, Ennio thinks. They haven't even got proper streets yet.

At the entrance to the village there is an alley, too narrow to let more than one person pass at a time. While squeezing through, a fat woman appears from nowhere, her face full of colour and so naturally overloaded she can't walk properly. She stares at the boy, surprised, asking herself who this stranger could possibly be.

She's fat, Ennio thinks, staring back at her. The description fits. Could she be his mother? He braces himself, prepares to be recognised.

'Is your name Ennio?' the woman says. He says yes just as she leaps forward to hug and kiss him.

'How are you my little *comparuccio*?' she says. Due to her use of that word, Ennio knows she is not his mother.

'Tell me who you are,' he says. 'I have been away for so long that I don't remember any more.'

'I am your godmother,' she explains. He can't remember ever seeing her before in his life, but to give the impression he hasn't forgotten, he improvises a line: 'Look how much weight you've put on,' he says, forcing a smile.

Calling her fat oddly enough makes the woman burst out laughing. Grabbing her stomach, she says: 'Yes it's true, I was slim before, but I slowly put on weight bit by bit to the point where I can't actually move any more.' She takes Ennio by the hand and leads him away. Swinging around, he just has time to wave goodbye to the postman, who gives him a sign as if to say good luck.

In his godmother's house he sits down, and is offered a glass of wine.

'There's no point getting me anything to eat as I had lunch with the school director,' he says. The godmother disappears for a few minutes, coming back with her husband, who literally smothers Ennio, he is so happy to see him. This must be his godfather, Ennio thinks, not recognising him either.

'Why have you come back to the village?' the man asks.

'I had had it up to here with college,' says Ennio. 'And I missed my mother. Given I haven't had any news from her in ages, that she hasn't shown any sign of life, I thought I would just show up.'

He asks where his mother is living, and godmother replies: 'Don't worry. You don't need to know. This is such a small village that word will get around so quickly and within minutes she will be here. You'll see.'

The husband fills Ennio's glass as soon as it is empty, and then the two insist he eats some sausage and parmesan cheese. As he is finishing off his plate he hears children outside making a racket. He looks up and sees a woman approaching, a fat woman, or rather quite a robust woman. She is tall with a sullen face and a fixed glare. Ennio is about to take another mouthful but puts the food down as she approaches.

'Mamma!'

With his emotions running in all directions and his heart in palpitations, Ennio searches for something to say. What can he say? Nothing meaningful comes, only confusion. He just stares as she comes through the door, but when she gets close the tears well up. He throws his arms around her neck.

The questions bubble back up to the surface and break through the blubbering.

'Mamma, mamma, you're alive. What happened? Why haven't you been in touch? Answer me so I can be happy again. It's great to see you! It must seem impossible to understand but I thought that my emotions had dried up. But now that you're here I feel there is someone in the world to care about. For how many years have I been sad? How I hate to look back at a mistake no-one even knows who made. Did I do you wrong? If so I beg you, please forgive me!

Hug me, please. I want to feel the feelings I haven't felt for so long. It's fantastic to be here again with you. I dreamt that one day I would see you again and now that day is here. How are you?'

After this speech the reservoir of words runs dry. Ennio cries some more with his arms wrapped around her and his head buried in her dress. Her eyes are also gleaming.

Looking up, he strokes her face and gives her a smile, which she reciprocates. He then leads her by the hand to a seat next to his godmother.

'What is more beautiful in the world than this?' Ennio asks, but his mother doesn't answer. In her face he reads satisfaction.

Mother and son stay in this house for about an hour, and then decide to leave when Ennio complains of tiredness. Outside, the sun is setting and he can only just make out the faces of the people he passes.

A group of men are playing *bocce* in the village square. Ennio looks each one in the face in the hope of recognising someone, but not one face is familiar. 'I've been away too long,' he says.

Mother points to one of them and says: 'He's your stepfather.'

'What exactly would that be?' Ennio asks. 'Is he your husband?' She nods.

At that moment the man turns around, sees mother, bids goodbye to his friends and approaches. As his profile becomes clearer, Ennio sees traits in him he doesn't like. To start with, he is too old for mother. He looks weak, wears glasses and smokes a pipe. He looks like a retired sailor.

'Nice to meet you, Signor Domenico is the name,' he says, stretching out a paw.

'Nice to meet you,' Ennio replies.

Domenico suggests they go home. Once there, he offers Ennio coffee. Examining him more closely, Ennio realises his first impressions might be mistaken. He is not as stupid as he looks, though Ennio still wonders what made his mother shack up with him. Now that he is present, she doesn't speak much at all. She just stares at Ennio in an odd, off-putting way.

The conversation about family and village affairs drags on, with people coming and going, including some who were Ennio's childhood friends. The prodigal son is now frightfully tired and asks to be excused. He kisses everyone and goes upstairs, falling asleep as soon as his head hits the pillow. His brain needs time to process all the new data it has amassed.

Mother wakes him the next morning with breakfast. He kisses her, happy to see her. 'Have you slept well?' they ask each other.

'Come out and see the village, see if it still is as you remember it,' she says.

They wander around. Ennio doesn't remember much at all. There is a spectacular view from the end of one of the streets, a view famous for miles around. He doesn't even remember that.

Then they go visiting. Mother's sister is first on the list. Her little daughter opens the door, she must be only three. *'Ciao Zia!'* she says to Ennio's mother, though upon seeing the strange boy she turns her eyes to the floor. Inside, mother greets her sister, who offers Ennio her hand. All three sit down and the two women begin to talk in the local dialect, which Ennio has forgotten. Mother then switches to Italian: 'Yes, he is my son.'

Ennio's aunt jumps up, elated in her turn. 'Ennio how are you?' she says between kisses and cuddles. 'I didn't recognise you. Look how big you are! You look as if you were a young man living in the city.'

Two more daughters then appear. The extended family sits around the fire, firing questions at Ennio, who begins to feel like a zoo attraction. Uncle arrives. He recognises his nephew immediately, approaches with an outstretched hand and says simply: 'Welcome.' It is a classy introduction, though he then spoils it by launching into the same set of questions.

This process repeats itself. Relatives, Ennio discovers he has quite a few, pop in to say hello with annoying frequency. 'Why don't we just call a village assembly?' Ennio thinks. He gets so bored that his mother notices. She signals to the throng that they should be going. Even on the way home strangers stop mother to ask who the boy is. Yet more questions.

Back safely behind a closed door, Ennio helps his mother prepare lunch. Over the main course he repeats the question he has asked himself so many times over the years: 'Mamma, why didn't you come to visit me?' She pretends not to understand. She wants to get away without answering, but that's not going to happen. Ennio asks until she answers.

'I was afraid to come because I didn't have any money and I thought that if I didn't pay them they would send you home,' she says.

Indignant, he answers back. 'So did you think it was best just to disappear for all that time? Or did you think that if no-one turned up they would feel pity for me and pay for my studies? Look mamma, people are slowly but surely waking up. No-one does charity work anymore, so get used to it. Do you know how many years of suffering, not to mention missed studies, I went through because of what you thought? More than three goddam years! How can I forget them? Do you realise that I missed three years' schooling just at a time when I was starting to do well? Out of the blue comes your decision to abandon me, a decision that ruins everything, just when I had started to plan for the future. Your childish ideas mean I have to start everything from scratch, and I suppose I can't count on you, what with the way you view life.'

Her feeble explanation angers him. He is about to get fired up a little more when the door opens and Graziano, his brother, comes in. Ennio drops the subject, though while Graziano is hanging up his coat, he whispers to mother: 'I want to continue this conversation another day.' She looks at him, saying nothing.

Routine sets in quickly. Every morning Ennio's stepfather makes coffee and takes it up to mother, who stays in bed until late, saying she is tired. Stepfather goes out to fetch wood and tends to his vegetable patch. In the evening they all sit around the fire, staring at each other.

Within three weeks Ennio is bored, and within three months he is miserable again. Over the summer he goes out on long hikes, rediscovering the mountain range with his childhood friends. But soon the days get shorter and he realises there will be nothing to do. Winter promises to be long and bitter.

What they said at the monastery was true. This village was godforsaken, especially when it snowed. Even walking, the main village pastime, was out of the question for most of the winter. Ever inventive and scratching around for any kind of activity, Ennio makes skis from two lengths of wood. This amuses the local kids, who have never heard of the sport.

Spring comes around. Ennio is now sixteen and wants to escape the village and its monotony. He wants a life of his own. He can't bear the thought of hanging around Morrea until he is officially deemed an adult and therefore old enough to do as he pleases.

'Why do you look so sad?' asks the local priest, when he finds Ennio sitting on a hilltop just outside the village.

'I want to go away,' Ennio says. 'I don't want to hang around here doing nothing, just waiting for divine providence to come down from the skies like everyone else does.'

'You need to be patient my son,' the priest says. 'God sees all and provides for all.'

Uncomfortable, Ennio stands, determined not to take any more of this nonsense. 'Everyone must try his own path,' he preaches to the priest. 'I'm not waiting around here for divine providence to arrive.' The priest, surprised, says nothing.

Spring becomes summer and Ennio is still in Morrea. On the first day of summer mother announces she is going to Rome to work in the fields, as many villagers do. She leaves as part of a group of between ten and twenty women, with one or two men thrown in for good measure. They head off towards Rome with the intention of touring the farms looking for work. Those who got lucky would perhaps pick potatoes, from early in the morning until midday, when it was too hot, and then again in the evening. It is hard work, and they have only Sundays free, when they choose some common point to meet up and gossip. In one or two months they earn enough to tide them over for the winter.

While the women are in the fields near Rome the men are at home working hard, looking after their own fields, and the kids. They usually get up before 6am.

After a summer away, the smallest kids sometimes don't remember their mother any more. They need to be reintroduced.

Ennio bumps into the priest another time over that summer. He can't resist having another dig. 'How long have these poor people been waiting for your divine providence?' Ennio chides. 'Do you like watching people suffer?' The priest gives Ennio a dirty look and walks away.

That evening, at home after dinner, he finds himself alone with his stepfather. Graziano is out playing with his friends. As stepfather settles down as usual with his pipe, Ennio seizes the chance to probe him about his mother.

'Why is it that she never came to visit me?' he asks.

'I suggested to her on more than one occasion that she visit you. But she was afraid of being asked for money for your studies.'

He tells Ennio how the two met. 'I escaped Rome when the Germans arrived, leaving all my worldly goods and all my money with my wife and children. When the war ended I went back and all of them, my wife and my children, refused to acknowledge me, refused to even look me in the face. I tried to talk them around, but when I left the house one day to look for petrol they slammed the door behind me and told me not to come back.' Soon after this he met Ennio's mother while working the fields, and they decided to live together in the village.

'I am your mother's victim,' he continues. 'It is difficult, due to my age, to get her to respect me. I have to do exactly what she wants, or I will get it in the neck. I don't have a single lira to my name. As soon as I earn anything your mother takes it from me. It's a sacrifice, but I put up with it because I love her.'

Ennio feels sorry for him. He is chained down, a prisoner like he was. He seems more human than his mother. His life is basically over and he is just waiting to die, to be released from the suffering surrounding him.

'If I had been free to decide I would have taken you out of school and would have let you choose the road you thought best,' the stepfather says.

The conversation moves on. 'Here in the village, every summer, the farmers who live in Rome come up to have a bit of a holiday,' Domenico says. 'They'll be here any day now and I'll introduce you to a few of them, one in particular: Cannolicchio. You'll see, someone will take you to Rome. There you can choose what you want to do. I see you're suffering here. If you don't go to Rome, you'll stay just the way you are for the rest of your life.'

Ennio spends the next two weeks working in the fields. In the evenings he crawls upstairs to bed, his arms and legs aching. As always, work is better than no work because it makes the days pass quickly.

One morning his stepfather wakes him with news. 'Do you remember the *signore* I was telling you about?' he asks. 'Well, he should be arriving today. If all goes well you'll be in Rome in two weeks.'

It turns out that the whole village is waiting for this *signore* to arrive, principally because he is the richest man for miles around. He looks about fifty-five and has a bald patch surrounded by long white hair he ties in a bun at the back. Glasses cover his beady eyes and leather trousers cover his boots.

As soon as Cannolicchio arrives the younger kids run up to him, asking to carry his bags. They are angling for a tip. He goes straight to his house, which was boarded up for the rest of the year.

That afternoon, just to show how much money he has, he walks around the village buying drinks for everyone he recognises.

From between the drawn curtains of his mother's front room, Ennio watches his stepfather take up a place on a bench in the village square beside Cannolicchio. From the way they talk they seem to know each other well, though Ennio knows nothing of their relationship.

A man approaches the bench. Cannolicchio holds out his hand, allowing himself to be greeted like royalty.

'Why not have a glass of wine?' he says.

The lucky recipient, a humble farmer like everyone else, feels so inferior, so unworthy, he does not dare sit at this rich man's table, choosing instead to sit three or four metres away, on another bench, to finish his drink.

As he leaves the farmer touches his cap and says *'grazie Cannolicchio'*. Cannolicchio waves his hand and continues his conversation with Ennio's stepfather. Ennio takes a good look at the man before going upstairs to lie on his bed and wait for the outcome.

At around 4pm the stepfather comes back and says: 'It looks like he has accepted, but he wants to see you, not now, because he's going to sleep, but later this evening. The guy's loaded so make sure he likes you and then you'll be fine. Did you see the way everyone comes to see him?'

The siesta hour over, they go back to the bar in the square. The stepfather introduces Ennio, stressing his good nature and so on.

'How do you do?' says Ennio, sitting down next to Cannolicchio while the stepfather continues with his persuasion. Ennio has no idea what Cannolicchio's business is. After the customary glass of wine, the stepfather tells Ennio to leave. He wants to close the deal. Ennio gets up, says goodnight, goes home and waits by the fire.

Two hours later the stepfather is back, tipsy and with a smile on his face. 'Cannolicchio has accepted you. Within a month you will be working for him in Rome.' Ennio is so happy he throws his arms around his stepfather and kisses him on the nose.

That night he dreams of the future with great things in store. The following days whiz by. He spends time on the hilltop taking in his last glimpses of the Abruzzo mountains, thinking about that incredible city, Rome, which lies behind them. Rome, where everyone dreams of going, but which none of these villagers has the courage to tackle head-on. For these poor people, Rome is just an abstract idea, a world full of unattainable riches.

Departure day arrives. Ennio does the rounds in the village, saying goodbye to his relatives. He is proud to tell them where he is going. They all say they are envious.

He walks down to the bus stop with his stepfather. The two take the four-hour journey together, arriving in the evening just as all the street lamps are being turned on. It is a marvellous sight. Rome is all lights and traffic. Ennio is still not used to cars and is scared of crossing the road. They stay in a hotel. The following morning his stepfather takes him to the shop where he will be working. On the way he points to the famous squares and churches. So much grandeur.

They arrive at the shop. Cannolicchio comes out to shake Ennio's hand.

'How do you like Rome?' he says.

'I like it, I think I like it a lot,' Ennio replies. Other boys of around his age came out of the shop, curious to see who has arrived.

He has escaped the countryside.

Part Two

'The advance has been halted for days. Why don't they move?' Derek asked the captain.

Dinner for five at *La Casita*, a small Saigon restaurant that despite its name served essentially French food.

'The basic reason,' the captain explained, 'is that they are no longer used to advancing. The Americans wanted to take on all the fighting, which meant there was nothing left but static defence for us. As well as that, it's the 21st division from the Mekong Delta on the highway. They feel a long way from their waterways, and swamps and rivers. They don't feel that involved.'

By the time they reached the main course the captain was the only sober diner. Dinner had been preceded by a cocktail party on the lawn of a boring French banker. The others at the table: Derek, the banker, Ennio and his wife Michelle, had had more than their fill of cocktails.

'You see!' said Michelle. 'If they don't care, why ever should I? Why should I mind who wins this goddam war?'

Michelle's neuroticism was verging on the hysterical, and with good reason. Since the simple marriage ceremony in the Italian consulate, people had been looking at her strangely. Her friends and even her relatives made comments about Ennio and his 'special friend' Derek.

She confronted her husband and even tried banning him from seeing the Englishman, but Ennio would simply shrug the whole affair off as ridiculous. 'You're crazy,' he would say. 'And in any case, I'll see whomever I choose.'

She became suspicious every time he left the house, every time he was sent into the field on a job. She demanded details, lists of all the colleagues he would be working with. Whatever information he gave, she was not satisfied.

She began checking the sheets whenever she came back to the apartment. At the back of her mind she knew, but she didn't know what to do.

That night, Ennio had come back from Kontum in the central highlands, a town recaptured by Saigon after a week of fighting. He had been showing Italian newsmen around, a profitable sideline because they came to Vietnam with wads of dollars.

The dinner party was discussing a siege by the North Vietnamese of a garrison at An Loc, northwest of Saigon. It had been going on for two months and the garrison refused to give in despite being short of both food and bandages. The soldiers had become heroes in the eyes of the South Vietnamese, who had by this time begun to despair of finding anyone who could stand up to the relentless surging army of children pushing down from the north.

There was a relief column advancing from the south with incredible slowness. They were making so little progress the foreign press would drive about an hour out of Saigon just to see how they were getting on. Everyone knew exactly where they would be; in the same spot as last time. It was 1972.

Michelle had another reason to be annoyed with the world. Her shop, or 'salon' as she called it, was not going well. Selling perfume in the middle of a war was not a particularly good idea, but Ennio was willing to do anything just to keep her occupied and therefore out of his hair. He had sunk a big chunk of his savings into the venture, and the money was evaporating.

'You're a trained first-aid worker,' the captain said to Michelle, his wife's sister. 'Just report to any casualty ward in Saigon and they will greet you like an angel. They're inundated.'

'What?' sneered Michelle, 'and tend to Vietnamese? To louts who can't even read? Who do you think I am?' She repeated herself: 'Who do you think I am?'

'I think you're Vietnamese yourself,' snapped the captain.

'No she's not! She's Italian now,' Derek interrupted sarcastically. 'She doesn't belong in Vietnam any more. What do you think she got married for?'

Michelle leant forward and slapped Derek ineffectually, hitting his large nose. She then shouted at Ennio: 'How can you let him treat me like that? Say something!'

Derek, by now numb to any drama that didn't involve multiple deaths, found the evolving scene amusing. He chuckled. The alcohol-fuelled Ennio chuckled too.

'He's right,' Ennio said, referring to the captain. 'Soldiers here are in a bad way. They need nurses. I've seen them bleeding to death just because there is no-one around to bandage them.' Ennio never defended his wife. He was fed up with her behaving like a spoiled brat.

Michelle wanted to involve the French banker. 'You see how he sides with him?' she said, referring to Ennio and Derek. 'You see how he backs this Englishman against me? Isn't it sweet? You'd be surprised what I know about these two.'

And then to Ennio: 'In fact I sometimes wonder whose husband he is…'

The Frenchman's turn to chuckle: '*Mais didons,*' he said.

Michelle wouldn't stop: 'Anyway, why should I care about this dreary war?'

The captain exploded: 'Because our families are in it, and have been for years, you ugly snob! I find your remark ungrateful, after what they've been through, presumably for your benefit. And what about your father? Isn't he a Vietnamese and a soldier? You're despicable.'

Michelle burst into tears. Ennio didn't react.

The captain went on: 'Since 1945, I've lost nine members of my family and I'm the last one. War has been our life. I am 34 but when I am killed, my sons will go on fighting after me, to avenge our family, the dead, and to defend our homeland. And she dares speak like that! How can she? Does she belong to our family or not? Have you forgotten who your family is? Aren't you the daughter of an army colonel? Or are you not? Who are you then?' He looked around the table. 'Who is this woman?'

Ennio, who had stopped chuckling, couldn't agree more. He thought it might be appropriate to back up the general sentiment by giving his wife a bloody nose. He started to raise his fist and lean towards her, but Derek saw him, grabbed his wrist and held his hand down against his leg.

'Did you know that it was a Briton, major general Douglas G Gracey, who started the Vietnam War?' Derek asked in an obvious attempt to change the subject. Everyone stared at him. Only Ennio had heard the story before.

'Yes, I'm absolutely serious,' Derek went on. 'Winston Churchill had sent General Gracey to Saigon to disarm the surrendered Japanese in 1945, but when he arrived he thought himself a war lord and began involving himself in business which had nothing to do with the British.

'Most importantly, he released 1,400 French troops who had been interned by Tokyo. They went on the rampage, raising the French flag and ran the Vietminh, the forerunners of the Vietcong, out of town. There was a general protest strike the next day, and that was the start of the conflict.'

'Is that so?' said the French banker, impressed.

But Michelle wasn't listening and wouldn't be diverted.

'We were at Edith Piaf's funeral in Paris together,' she said in her best Italian-French mock accent. 'When we were in Paris, we went on a holiday to Rhodes and rode around on donkeys... he knows a countess in Rome... as the BBC correspondent, he does this that and the other... I hear this all the time you know.'

She stared at Derek's hand, which was still holding down Ennio's.

'Just look,' she said to the banker with disgust on her face. And then to Ennio: 'Why don't you give your friend a kiss as well while you're about it? It wouldn't be the first time.'

'Shut up,' said Ennio.

'Shut up yourself,' she replied, still mocking his accent.

'Have you gone mad? We are in company now,' Ennio said.

'I don't care,' she said. 'Let the whole of Saigon know.'

Derek again chimed in, unhelpfully: 'Well, if he won't give me a kiss, I'll give him one,' at which he gave Ennio a smacker on the cheek, adding: 'Anyone else?'

The banker laughed a little, but he was looking stressed.

Michelle mumbled to herself. 'It's him he really loves,' she said. 'I only come second. They snatch meetings behind my back every time they can.'

'We're going home,' Ennio told her, attempting to yank her up from her seat. But she wouldn't budge. She stayed slumped over her chair, makeup stains all over her face. She started to wail like a baby who hadn't been fed.

'I don't know where he was last night,' she cried.

'I told you. I was in a bunker outside Kontum with Italian television men. I was showing them around,' he said, but it was no use. Something was broken that couldn't be fixed.

Michelle started blowing her nose. 'Are you sure, or was it a bunk in Saigon?' she said.

Ennio decided he wasn't going to take any more. He stood up and knocked his wife right off her seat. It was a backhander, not a bad shot.

Michelle dragged herself up to the table by her fingertips. She looked at all those present one by one, for just a second. Instead of retaliating she kept on calmly addressing the banker, blood running from her nose.

'Do you know where they met?' she asked. 'At a bus stop in Rome, late at night. Ennio at the time was a shoeshine boy.'

The marriage was over, Ennio realised. It had lasted just two months.

*

Part Three

'Contemplating the glories of ancient Rome, waiting for a bus, or sheltering from the rain?'

It was the summer of 1960 when Derek saw Ennio leaning against a bus shelter near Piazza Navona. Derek, lanky with blond hair and a horse-like nose, was twenty-seven. Ennio was nineteen.

None of these three suggestions was correct, as it turned out. That night, Ennio had discovered that his girlfriend was a whore. He had caught her in bed with a fat, bald man. She had told him she was a waitress. Rather than anger him, the discovery depressed him. After three years in Rome he thought he had become a streetwise operator. Getting duped by a girl even younger than himself made him feel like a wide-eyed country bumpkin just off the bus from the Abruzzo.

Adding to the depression was the fact that he was now homeless. Before storming out he had given both the girl and the fat man a good kick in the stomach. Unfortunately for Ennio, he was living in her apartment and had nowhere else to stay.

Cannolicchio had turned out to be a big disappointment. Ennio had heard about his 'shop' but had no idea what trade Cannolicchio was actually in, and therefore had no idea what he would be doing when he got to the big city. Cannolicchio was a shoeshine baron. He controlled all the shoeshine business south of Termini railway station and brought new boys in from the countryside every year.

Ennio was immediately given his own corner and instructed to hand over half of anything he made. Accommodation, a mattress, was provided for the best part of a year. Then, when the next wave of boys began to arrive – all from the Abruzzo, and a couple from Morrea – he was told to fend for himself.

What kind of deal did his stepfather do with Cannolicchio? Ennio mused while polishing the shoes of politicians and clergy. An introduction fee? How many boys had he put on the conveyor belt to Rome?

He developed his own little call and learnt from the other boys to attract attention by knocking his brush against his box of polish. He didn't care at first, as living in Rome was mind-blowing. If the sun was shining, which was most of the time, he knew he didn't need money to have fun. It was an open-air museum. He spent his spare time wandering around, imagining that he was an emperor, the owner of all the monuments he came across.

Pinching the rears of the American women and fleecing tourists of any nationality became his sidelines. Fleecing, however, was risky as the police didn't appreciate boys from the country. They gave pickpockets a crack over the head and a *foglio di via*, a sheet of paper ordering the holder to leave the city within forty-eight hours. After the third warning, Ennio decided to leave the tourists alone. He feared the police would break his skull.

So when Cannolicchio turned him out, money became a pressing concern. The fifty-fifty financial arrangement still applied, and any sign of rebellion was put down with a bared blade.

Worse still, he soon discovered polishing shoes did not impress the women. Decent girls avoided him like the plague as soon as they saw polish under his fingernails. Only the rough women, outsiders and often from the south, would entertain the idea of being seen with a shoeshine boy from the Abruzzo. Some were half-decent girls in service in the posh houses; cleaners, kitchen helps or baby-nurses. Others were waitresses, whores, or thieves, and some did a little of everything. It was difficult to tell who was who.

The rough girls did have their uses. They introduced Ennio to tricks. The stories they told of easy money were too amazing to ignore. If one girl had a guy on her hook she could do whatever she wanted, even take money out of his wallet right in front of him. The girls said they knew boys who earned just as much as they did. Lots of the clients were in the church.

So he got in on the act. He did tricks to survive, he told himself. Was he supposed to live on *ciabatta* and nothing else? he said, if anyone asked him why. In any case, what was so bad about biting pillows? He didn't enjoy it, but it beat shining shoes or cleaning greasy pans, that was for sure.

He had made it to Rome and was determined to keep moving up in the world, even if it meant sleeping around. The combined income of tricks and shoe-shining wasn't enough to rent an apartment by himself, but it usually kept him from begging or stealing. He mostly dossed in friends' rooms.

That night, the first night, Derek took him to a place just around the corner from the bus shelter, on Piazza Lancellotti. Nothing happened. Ennio was exhausted and fell asleep straight away. Derek, at this stage still the perfect gentleman (he went around Rome saying 'sorry' and 'thank you' all the time) didn't dare wake Ennio for sex – that would have been rude.

Reinforcing this quintessential Englishman image was his insistence on telling the truth and never scheming or swindling. He was, he said, 'a man of principle'. It was not the kind of attitude that gets one far in the Italian capital. Most of the Romans thought he was quaint at best, if not plain stupid.

So Ennio took advantage. Derek was still a closet gay and would remain so for another thirty years. Italy was not as homophobic as Britain, but Derek refused, sometimes violently, to be defined by his occasional sexual preferences. Even when it was explained to him that no-one really cared in Italy, that many boys experimented and some did it with other boys out of necessity, Derek didn't want to know. He lashed out whenever anyone called him gay.

Meeting Ennio meant Derek could tap into his real self. It was Derek's first relationship and Ennio, using skills picked up from his girlfriends, soon had him on a leash. Derek had not even spent the whole night with a 'boy' before.

To start with, Ennio milked the sob story about the lying whore, without having to exaggerate much. He said he needed a friend. After that first night of just sleeping, Ennio suggested another meeting. Derek's eyes lit up.

They met the next night, and the next. They soon developed a routine. Ennio would phone Derek's apartment from the bar across the road, letting it ring twice and then putting the phone down. Derek would come to the balcony and toss down the keys to the front door.

There was no reason, in Ennio's opinion, why he shouldn't let Derek know he was poor. Over dinner in the *rosticcerie* he complained about his shirt's frayed cuffs, his shabby jeans, and his ailing mother who needed medicine. Some of it was true, and in any case Ennio felt no guilt. A girl, he knew, would have behaved just the same. Derek had to pay for his pleasure.

As for the sex, he put up with it but never pretended to like it. He trained himself to think about something else while Derek had his wicked way. 'I'm not even here,' he told himself. While Derek humped, Ennio plotted new ways to get into his wallet.

Derek fell for him hard, and for a while the Italian could do anything he wanted. But after a few weeks he was found out.

On the road to Fiumicino airport, which was under construction at that time, Derek had a puncture. He had been tasked with writing a feature for his employer, the Reuters news agency, and had taken Ennio along as a translator.

They had a spare, but neither of them could get the flat tire off. This was already embarrassing for Ennio, who had told Derek he was a mechanic (shoeshine boy was too humiliating). The shame was compounded when the *carabinieri* turned up and pointed out the hubcap was still on.

Derek said nothing, but the next day he went looking for Ennio's non-existent garage. He found his new friend hard at work over a man's boot.

'Why didn't you tell me?' Derek asked.

'Because I thought you'd be ashamed of me,' said Ennio.

To his amazement, he got away with it. Derek felt sorry for him, all the more so after Ennio threw in choice details about his pitiful childhood. At one stage Derek had to wipe away a tear.

So Ennio began to up the stakes.

The next goal was a scooter. 'I need to visit my sick mother during siesta,' he said. After initial protest and despite a price tag equivalent to two months' wages, Derek agreed.

But this scam fell through as well because Derek didn't have the residency documents needed for the hire-purchase agreement. It was quite a scene. They actually threw him out of the showroom when they found out he wasn't a Rome resident.

So Ennio moved on to another target. He suggested they live together. 'We could be together at any time of day or night,' he told Derek. 'It would be all over with nights at Palazzo Lancelotti and my sneaking in. We would be free of all that. My cousin Giorgio could find us a flat.'

Giorgio introduced Derek to a woman who showed them around a place in Parioli. She asked for three months' rent in advance.

Derek wasn't keen. 'Parioli's too far out of town,' he said.

'But we'd have a room to ourselves,' Ennio protested.

'A room? But there are two rooms here,' Derek pointed out.

'Giorgio will have the other.'

'And who's going to pay his rent?' Derek asked.

'Well… you, I suppose.'

Derek's face grew grey. He threw a ten lire coin in Ennio's face and told him to fuck off.

Derek thought Ennio was trying to pull the wool over his eyes by moving in without telling him he had to pay Giorgio's rent. In reality, the scam was much better than that. The flat was vacant property and the woman who showed them around had no connection with the owner. She would have simply pocketed the advance, and if anyone showed up Giorgio and Ennio were planning to do a runner, leaving Derek to face the police.

Giorgio and Ennio were a team. Giorgio was Cannolicchio's right-hand man, and the two were always looking out for scams more sophisticated than just pick-pocketing tourists.

The scooter idea was a rip off too, though Derek never knew. If he had managed to buy one, Ennio and Giorgio would have stolen it from him and sold it.

When these plans didn't come off, Ennio changed tack once again. Realising by instinct alone that Derek appreciated honesty, he admitted to his wrongdoings and asked for forgiveness.

Derek was quite angry. 'What are you telling me this for, and why now?' he said. 'It's over between you and me.'

'I've broken up with Giorgio,' Ennio said.

'Why? You were a good team. You'll easily find somebody else. You have a nice act – all that being timid and lost and then falling asleep.' Derek now suspected Ennio had been leading him on since the very first night.

'I know you won't believe me,' Ennio said. 'Why should you? But it's true. I've never been with a man before. You're the first…'

Derek laughed.

'You don't know why I'm telling you this, do you?'

'Of course I do,' Derek said. 'Giorgio has got a plan for fleecing me again. I'm one of your fools. What's your proverb? When fools sleep, the bright boys don't eat?'

'We had some good times together. I want to be with you again. You behaved like a gentleman towards me. I feel like a grain of salt. I want to ask you to forgive me. I told Giorgio I was leaving him for you. He slapped me on both cheeks. Hard. You can see the marks. Then he got hold of my collar from behind and pulled me down on the street and started kicking, really hard, and shouting. A police car passed and stopped and he ran away. Good riddance.

'What a fool I was! To think that I couldn't tell the difference between you and him. He's a shit. Forgive me. Please!'

Ennio had told a lot of lies in his time, but convincing Derek to believe all this after the pranks he had pulled was hard work, even when up against a relative pushover. There were always elements of truth in good lies, he knew, so he threw in a few. He had actually fallen out with Giorgio, for example.

And he was growing to like Derek, though at first he didn't know why. At the beginning and despite the age gap he considered the journalist nothing more than a little boy with a lot of learning to do. In terms of his personal development, Derek was in Ennio's eyes the schoolboy back in the dorm who had just come across two naked boys in bed. Superficially, Ennio projected a man-of-the-world image. The only missing element was money.

'Why did you pick on me in the first place?' Derek asked.

'Giorgio followed us one night. He thought you were an easy touch. You foreigners live in a cow's belly here. Foreigners always leave. We wanted to pluck your feathers before you left too.'

After working on him for a few hours, Ennio noticed Derek was starting to give in again. 'Call tomorrow before the end of my shift,' Derek said.

Over the next week there were a couple of brush-offs. When Derek saw Ennio waiting outside the office entrance he walked by, pretending not to see. But he was lonely and couldn't keep resisting for long. Soon they we were eating dinner together again.

Within weeks the couple moved into a grim one-bedroom flat near Piazza del Popolo. It had two iron beds and damp walls. Ennio was happy with Derek's sign of commitment. He felt looked after. Derek was also happy, though he didn't know it.

The cohabitation was not without danger. The bosses at Reuters were pompous, judgmental and unlikely to be understanding of such a liaison, Derek presumed. Given what happened later, this presumption proved spot on.

The working mentality at Reuters was still colonial. The Italians were considered Indians, unsophisticated and corrupt.

The disrespect was mutual. For many Italians these English pressmen were silly pricks who wore dull clothes and spent all day pointlessly talking about how they hated adjectives.

According to Derek's training, adjectives were 'the work of the devil'. Facts on the other hand, were the 'bricks of civilisation'. It was all weird stuff.

After a few weeks Ennio discovered their new relationship was not actually the only one. Derek had a girl named Ginette; at this point he still indulged in women too.

When he found out, Ennio approved. His respect for Derek even increased a little, though keeping out of the way while Ginette was in Rome was annoying.

'She's just a friend,' Derek said, though this definition of their relationship no longer applied when he got her pregnant. At least, Derek thought it might have been him. Ginette was not too fussy about her partners after a few gins and tonics. Several of Derek's acquaintances had enjoyed her too, so together they chipped in for a back-street abortion. She tried to get Derek to marry her. 'Please, if only for my parents. I don't even expect a ring,' she wrote. Derek consulted with his mother and wrote back: 'Abort yourself.'

It was not, he knew, a very gentlemanly thing to do, but Ennio by this time had become something of a fixture. Derek was enjoying himself, and there was no way he was going to give up this new sensuous lifestyle.

Ennio was inserted into the ex-pat party circuit. He was never introduced by anything more than his name, and Derek delighted in the slow-burning scandal caused when acquaintances gradually realised they were an item. Before long Derek was flaunting his 'boy' without caring who knew.

The British thought Derek had come to Rome to do what he couldn't do at home, while the Italians didn't really care. No Italian would dare make a point of principle in public, or at least not outside church. Who cares what two people get up to in their bedroom?

Ennio enjoyed having the door opened on a new, luxurious world. He had never before been to a party where booze was so plentiful they stacked it on tables and left you to help yourself. His sidekick role was however not without its frustrations; it restricted his ability to chase women. He nevertheless decided this was an inconvenience worth putting up with for the short term. He could always visit girlfriends during the day while Derek was working, often with money taken from Derek's wallet. Even Derek's mother thought Ennio was good news. 'She would have been jealous of any female rival,' Derek explained.

Things went from good to better when Ennio landed a job. After hanging around with the Reuters bunch for long enough he was nominated 'runner' for the agency's special Olympic Games office, set up in a former monastery, the Domus Pacis. Derek's boss, who had his eye on Ennio and was suspicious of his employee's relationship, was too posh to worry about sport, so the arrangement slipped in under the radar.

The journalists sent over from Britain all thought the Italian was great fun. They would shout 'snap' after someone won a gold medal, and Ennio would run with the dispatch to the telex operators. Seconds counted. He taught the visitors the few words of mountain dialect he knew. They taught him the bizarre sport of cricket, using pinecones to explain the positions on the field. In the evenings they would go out to the *trattorie* and get hammered. Ennio would sing *Volare* like the stereotyped Italian everyone wanted him to be.

But before anyone could bask in social stability, Derek was told he was to be posted to Brussels. He hadn't even been in Rome a year and therefore thought of the move as a demotion. Few people had heard of the European Economic Community, and fewer still wanted to know more about it, especially in Britain.

He racked his brain but couldn't figure out why they were sending him off to the frozen north. He wondered whether he was being punished for his daring relationship. If that were the case, the managers at Reuters were not big enough to say so.

Ennio didn't take the news stoically. He remembered what he had been told – that foreigners seldom stayed in Rome. He knew this would probably apply to Derek too, but he was shocked it had come so soon.

The two were in bed drinking Chianti when Derek broke the news. Ennio cried and snivelled but then sobered up in no time when Derek said he wanted the two of them to move to the Belgian capital together.

'Are you having me on or something?' Ennio said.

'Why, what is the matter?' asked Derek.

'To get the mule to move, oil the wheels,' Ennio told him.

'What's that supposed to mean?'

'It means people have to be offered something. Can't you think what?'

'What are you talking about?'

Derek had no idea just how difficult it was to get a passport in Italy. In addition to the certificate of good conduct from the police you needed one from the doctor proving you were not about to export Italian diseases. Married men needed the consent of their wives. And worst of all, it was almost impossible to get one if you were male and of military service age, because the authorities presumed (rightly) that you wanted to run away in order to avoid serving your time.

If this was your case, the only solution was to pull a few strings with the police chief, or perhaps the bishop. If, that is, you had any strings to pull. Failing that you needed a lot of money. One leg shorter than the other was also an advantage, or at least a doctor's certificate saying you had. It was, without exaggeration, a nightmare.

Despite the obstacles and with typical British never-say-die, Derek tried to get a passport for Ennio. He soon found he couldn't do it on his own, but he found someone who could. An Italian journalist, a crime reporter working on a Rome newspaper, the *Messaggero*, came up with the brilliant idea of getting Ennio's mother to certify herself as dependent. That way, he wouldn't have to do his military service. It was a stroke of genius.

So together they struggled back up the mule tracks to Morrea in Derek's beaten up Morris Minor to see mamma. It was the first time Ennio had been back in three years, and it hadn't changed a bit.

Throughout the entire journey Derek pestered his passenger with questions about the valley, the river Liri, and Ennio's non-existent father. 'Why are journalists such a pain?' Ennio ended up asking.

'What the hell are you doing here?' was his mother's greeting when she saw the two of them.

'*Ma*, I'm going with this journalist to Brussels,' said Ennio without bothering with formalities.

Not knowing the name of any city outside Italy, she replied simply: 'Where? What do you want to go there for?'

'To find work, to learn things. Everybody's moving today. To Milan, to Turin…'

'What's wrong with Cannolicchio's?' mother asked.

'Did you want me to be a shoeshine boy all my life?' Ennio asked. 'Who do you think I am? I've quit.'

'Go then!' she shouted angrily.

'But mamma, we need you…'

'I'm staying here. You'll have to learn to cook on your own…' She suspected the two men wanted to take her to Brussels as their personal chef.

Ennio tried telling her about the form he needed her to sign, but it was difficult to get her to listen. She just stared at Derek and made dinner.

So Derek had a go. 'Signora Iacobucci, this evening is very important,' he said. 'By signing the form tomorrow, you will change the whole life of your son. Here he is on poor soil. He will not grow.

But if you sign, he will grow like a vine on a slope facing the sun…' Derek thought he would win the old lady over with poetry. It was a mistake; he should have gone directly for the money.

'What is this Brussels place?' mother asked, paying no attention to the patter. While Derek floundered around for more pretty words, she got down to business.

'That one has never sent me a lira!' she said, pointing at her son.

'If he gets to Brussels he'll send you five thousand a month,' Derek said. They haggled for a while and the deal was done after Derek agreed to put his pledge down in writing.

The next morning they descended the valley to the mayor's office, mother on a mule and the men following in the car. The mayor stamped and witnessed the required form and read out the financial pledge. Mother seemed happy.

Years later over some drunken dinner Derek would claim Ennio's mother sold him, but this was just his British way of seeing things. It was a deal to survive, to live a little better; a business deal. It is what anyone in her position in Italy would have done.

While that signature was the main hurdle, actually getting the passport took another six weeks of bureaucracy.

Ennio hung around in Rome, queuing in public offices, while Derek went ahead to Belgium.

Derek would much later become an expert on Rome, Italy and its way of life, publishing several editions of a guidebook and writing columns for a local newspaper. In his fifties and sixties, while living with Ennio's ghost, he would advise others on how best to deal with bureaucrats. He refined the process to an art. But when he left Rome for the first time he was still unused to the frustrations. The Englishman in him couldn't understand why the passport was taking so long.

In his newfound Belgian loneliness he blamed Ennio and told him so in regular missives. 'Delays cannot last forever,' he warned in one of them. 'Do you really want to come to Brussels, or is this all just a ploy to extract cash from me?'

Derek's mood swings were visible in his correspondence. In one postcard, clearly written while drunk from some Brussels bar late in the night, he regretted his admonishments. On one side, a night scene, neon ads for Tuborg and Dubonnet reflecting in the rain of a broad boulevard. On the other: 'I feel bad about hurting you because I need you a lot. We both need each other. With the world as it is, with that madman Khrushchev in Moscow, we'll go under if we stay alone. Together we are, and always will be, winners. Together we are strong.'

Ennio noticed the cold as soon as he got off the train. And the wet. To make his arrival just that bit more depressing, the restaurants didn't even serve spaghetti. It was a culture shock.

They didn't think much of two young men living together in Belgium either. Their first landlady trembled when Derek introduced Ennio. 'I will have nothing to do with your sheets!' she screamed in French with a hand clamped over her eyes, stamping her feet.

Neither did Derek's new boss at Reuters think much of Ennio. A fat man with a white moustache who drove a Chevrolet, he got so drunk every evening after work he could never find where he had parked it the next morning.

Lit up one night in a restaurant, he made some sarcastic comment to Derek about how 'provocative' they both were.

The cool welcome left Ennio with the impression his stay in Brussels would be short, but gradually people got used to him.

The landlady, who put money before principles, gradually calmed down and did end up washing sheets. The fat man's change of heart was even more remarkable. He found Ennio a job.

He became office boy for Gavin Gordon, a pleasant chap who wrote for the British newspaper The *Daily Telegraph*. It was, Ennio decided, a great job. All he had to do was pick up handouts from the ministries, rush cables to the post office and run errands for Gavin's wife Peggy. If things were quiet he would get asked to make coloured graphs explaining the European Steel and Coal Community, the embryo of the European Economic Community. Each country was to be highlighted using a different colour.

Putting on the Italian charm topped with lashings of the winning smile, Ennio soon had the couple eating out of his hand. Within the bat of an eyelid they were inviting him around to lunch every day, though given English cuisine, dumplings in particular, he did not count this as one of the better perks. They did however teach him how to type, and his English improved a lot. They both corrected Ennio very patiently: 'I have been in Belgium *for* six months, not *since* six months, Ennio,' Peggy would say time and time again until he got it right.

Ennio picked up languages instinctively, without knowledge of grammar. He had the gift and enjoyed it, becoming fluent in both French and English, though he could never master Vietnamese. Speaking another language allowed him to adopt another persona. He could forget for a moment his peasant Abruzzo upbringing. He could pretend, for example, to be a sophisticated intellectual from the Left Bank – a successful ploy with the ignorant girls back in Rome.

And once he had a job, Derek stopped treating him as if he were a cripple. The two became equals and their relationship improved no end. They were both outsiders in a tiny surreal country with its funny drunkards and blonde women with large breasts. Neither fitted in. In the evening they would tell each other stories and analyse the news. It was neutral territory, and Ennio felt things were working out.

In Brussels they got their first taste of political violence. The country was on the verge of economic collapse because it had been made to give up its colony, the Congo, as well as the Congo's cash cow, the copper mines. The Belgian workers were rioting.

From the terrace of a colleague's apartment, Ennio and Derek looked down as workers stoned portraits of the newlywed King Badouin and his Spanish bride Fabiola. 'Badouin to the gallows', they shouted (what does 'gallows' mean, Ennio asked?)

'Down with the Spanish cow!'

The mounted police were having none of it. They ploughed into demonstrators swinging their sabres. It took Ennio two weeks to get over the shock of seeing one man lose his hand. He had begun to see a world so much larger than his inbred, incestuous Italian region.

The 'lovers' would have no doubt settled down if it weren't for a rat. He was an English reporter sent to Belgium for the royal wedding. Derek, with Ennio in the car, gave him a lift one day and he saw a square locket with photos of the two of them with their arms around each other dangling from the dashboard. Derek had forgotten to remove it.

He definitely saw it, they decided afterwards, because from that ride onwards he had disgust in his eyes. Ennio learnt a new word, the stranger was, as Derek put it, 'the squealer'.

Derek knew someone must have squealed because he was posted back to what he would always call 'terrible London' for no known reason, once again before the end of his contract.

Ennio was pleased with the prospective move. 'At last, London,' he said. 'A decent city where Italians can earn money and be someone.' After less than a year and despite the welcome he had been given by Gordon and Peggy, who had already become like family, he was fed up with grey, wet, bland Brussels.

Derek, who hated his own people, the English, was also forced to admit there were advantages; the relationship would be more difficult to spot in the crowd.

Ennio rejoiced. He knew the weather would be no better in London, but thought the capital meant moving upwards.

And while outwardly supportive of Derek and his career, deep down Ennio longed for a blonde of his own. With money in London he might get one, he thought. He had been putting up with the filthy feeling of having a man's hands all over him for too long. He was allowed to flirt and gaze but he was still somebody's property while he couldn't fend for himself. He wasn't looking to get rid of Derek, whom he considered a decent friend. Nobody had helped him more. But he desperately wanted to be free. To a certain extent London brought the connotations of freedom usually associated with America. It would be the place where he could break loose, he believed.

In the event, that's not how it worked out.

They did a runner from the Brussels flat early in the morning without paying the last month's rent and set off for the Channel in the 'Bomber,' as they nicknamed their flash American car. It had windows like an aircraft and aerodynamic fins.

In Dover they were stopped. Customs officials wondered what on earth an Englishman with an international driving licence issued in Rome was doing in an American car with Belgian number plates, travelling with an Italian on a tourist visa. 'What do you intend to do in London?' they asked Ennio, who had not yet learnt the word 'intend'.

'Fancy a little tourism?' said the official sarcastically. 'Off to see the Tower of London?'

Noticing that Ennio had not heard of the Tower of London, they became more suspicious. 'How am I supposed to have heard of these places?' Ennio asked Derek later. 'When you're from Morrea, even the Spanish steps in Rome seem a million kilometres away.'

The border police took both men to a hut. They were held firmly by the arm so they wouldn't be tempted to make a break for it. Their bags were searched.

When in separate rooms, they told different stories. Ennio was questioned in Italian and immediately began to lie. He invented a story about travelling with his friend and wanting to see London. 'Such an amazing city, I'm told,' he said. 'I want to see the monuments, but to be honest I'm more interested in the clothes.'

In the other room Derek messed things up. He said Ennio would be helping his sickly mother with the housework – the worst possible answer. Ennio was deported immediately on the grounds that he was entering Britain to work without a permit. They put him on the next ferry to Dunkirk.

He did finally get into the country a couple of weeks later, but even then it was touch-and-go. Derek this time procured the necessary work visa, again using the sickly mother story. This plot would no doubt have run smoothly if Ennio had destroyed the letter as he had been instructed to do. 'The job in Scarborough will only be an excuse to get you into the country,' Derek wrote the previous week.

They searched Ennio a second time at Dover and found the incriminating evidence. They would have deported him a second time too had Derek not arrived in the nick of time, producing as if by miracle a separate letter from his mother proving that she was indeed in need of help in the house. Housework was 'beyond her,' it said.

'Please explain to me why I should let him in?' said the border officer.

‘My mother really does need help. The letter was to lure him over. Read this, officer,’ Derek said, waving the envelope under his nose.

On the long drive north, Derek gave Ennio the silent treatment.

Scarborough is not exactly London, and living with Derek’s mother soon became a drag. She and her friends ‘broke my balls,’ Ennio would recall years later. The endless cries of ‘what a beautiful day’ and ‘oh dear, oh dear’ were grating. Mother Wilson watched over Ennio as he did the chores, criticising any little mistake.

He was quickly depressed by the return to slave labour. It was as if he was back in the school canteen. He was also alone. Derek had sauntered off to London, and the Reuters head office, where he worked as a sub-editor.

In a letter to Derek he wrote: ‘What with your mother’s moaning and her awful, chewy steak-and-kidney pie, I would have lost my mind if it wasn’t for finding a job with Roberto Jacomelli, Scarborough’s ice cream king.’

It was technically an illegal job, but this was no real issue. Using his experience of menial labour and his natural charm he manipulated his co-workers to the extent that soon after getting taken on he could lounge away the whole day doing very little at all. ‘There are idiots here willing to do the work for me,’ he explained in another letter.

He would have been stuck in Scarborough much longer if it was not for ‘the adorable Mr Lee’ from the Home Office.

The pipe-smoking ‘little sod,’ as he otherwise became known, would come round to Derek’s mother’s place to spy on Ennio on the suspicion he was not actually helping out as he claimed. When he was working at the ice cream parlour, mother would cover for him. ‘He’s gone for a walk,’ she usually said. After hearing this excuse a few times, the little sod got angry. It began to look as if he wouldn’t renew Ennio’s visa.

These were anxious times for all concerned. Ennio became more and more desperate while mamma Wilson became hysterical. ‘I’m a bundle of nerves,’ she kept saying. ‘I feel rotten. I’m on the verge of a nervous breakdown.’

As the date of the visa renewal approached the two began avoiding each other so as not to bring the conversation up. ‘Without a visa and without you I'm just a rag, a worthless refugee,' Ennio told Derek on the phone. Visas are pieces of paper that mean little when you have them, but if you don't have them, they mean everything.

The poor old girl did end up having a breakdown. They had to take her to Scarborough General due to her 'palpitations'.

Shortly after, Ennio was told he was to be 'requisitioned'. He had no idea what the word meant. It sounded like some kind of torture. Derek explained he was being given a choice; leave the country or agree to a live-in job in London. He was to become a handyman at a London County Council hostel for the homeless in Swiss Cottage.

While everyone initially thought this was bad news, Mr Lee had actually done Ennio a great favour.

Swiss Cottage meant mending the boiler, mopping up and running errands, but that was infinitely better than watching Mrs Wilson fret over a cup of tea. Scarborough had become unbearable.

Ennio was put to work with the housekeeper, who was as blind as a bat without her glasses and who wore skirts so thick you would have thought they were bulletproof. He set about charming her, and it didn't take long. Within a few weeks she was cooking him jam tarts, which he generously pronounced to be one of England's more edible dishes. He taught her to say '*Buongiorno Signor Iacobucci*' when she saw him first thing in the morning.

A couple of months later she invited him into her room and with a giggle took his shirt off. 'She's not really up to my standards, but you mustn't be impolite, right?' Ennio told Derek over a half-pint. 'She's got saggy breasts and a backside which is so big it's difficult to find where it ends. Still, you have to keep in practice, don't you? At least she is willing.'

Derek moved into a bed-sit in Merton Rise, not far away. Ennio would go around during his afternoon break to take English lessons. His level of fluency improved so quickly Derek apologised for having underrated his friend. 'Just think what I could have become if I had had a proper education,' Ennio said. He also worked on his handwriting, which was still rough because he hadn't written much since the age of eleven.

They were still poor. Derek had to send money to both his own mother and to Ennio's, as he had promised. As a result Ennio was forced to eat at the hostel, which meant disgusting cabbage much of the time.

But twice a week, on his nights off, he would go down to the pub with Derek to drink warm beer. Over two half-pints each, Derek would talk about what it meant to be an existentialist, about how life was 'for kicks,' for fun.

The philosophy left Ennio cold. Kicks as far as he was concerned meant one thing: Gordon Snell's bottle parties on Saturday nights.

The British drinking tradition at first seemed bizarre. While he could hold his drink better than most Italians, he couldn't understand why the British wanted to drink to excess, to the extent that they lost all control. 'If you're out of control you look stupid, and your brain goes soft, too soft sometimes to move in on a woman if there is an opening,' he argued.

He slowly got into the spirit, however, though he never learnt to appreciate warm beer. Soon he was putting on drunken performances for Gordon, Derek, and their group of high-flying friends.

They would tease him by constantly asking if he was a 'Latin lover'. They never seemed to tire of renditions of *Volare* or *Roma nun far la stupida stasera.* They appreciated these songs so much they would scream collectively when Ennio let out the first note, much to his bemusement.

He appreciated them too. They were decent people and never looked down on him. But all the time he knew they were going places he could only dream of. One wanted to be a judge, another a theatre director. One even wanted to be a full-time poet.

'You want to reach the summit of journalism, and your friend will be a big name in the law courts,' Ennio told Derek one Saturday night. 'All of you have a future mapped out in your head. What have I got?'

'Everyone can have a future,' Derek said with a stammer. 'Everyone who wants a future can have a future. If you want a future you can have one as well. But not everyone wants a future, so there's space left for you.'

Ennio was doubtful. 'What can I do? Sweep the floor of the hostel until I'm dead?'

‘You can do a lot,’ Derek insisted. ‘Why don’t you try journalism? I could show you how to write an article that would interest Italy and then we could offer pieces to newspapers in Rome.’

‘You’re having me on,’ said Ennio.

‘It can be done. Think of it. Your name in print!’

‘You’re asking for the moon in the well,’ Ennio said. Derek didn’t understand the Italian proverb.

‘What’s that supposed to mean?’

‘You can see the reflection of the moon at the bottom of a well. But can you touch it? Can you hold it? You are asking for the impossible, that’s what it means,’ Ennio explained.

*

Ennio was glad to see the back of London too by the time he left. The partying was fun but the cabbage diet made him permanently sick, or so he believed. And apart from Derek’s friends, the locals all looked like victims, dressed in their monotonous greys and browns. Like Derek, the Londoners ran around saying ‘sorry’ and ‘thank you’ all the time. He thought them a little pathetic.

And the Home Office just wouldn’t leave him alone. Officials would turn up to turf him out of bed at dawn, asking stupid questions like ‘where is your boyfriend?’ He was amazed they took his relationship with Derek so seriously.

The British pretended to hate gays, he learnt, but when no-one was looking quite of few of them were at it in toilets and phone boxes. Once, two men pinned him against the wall of a phone box and tried to get his gear out of his jeans. He gave one of them an elbow in the face and wriggled clear. ‘You can’t afford me,’ he said, turning back as he ran down the street.

It was thanks to Ennio to a large degree that they decided to skip town. He saw an advert for a sub-editor in Paris with Agence France Presse in the magazine of the National Union of Journalists.

By this time, Derek was desperate to get out as well. Reuters had found out about the Brussels runner, and he was broke after having to fork out a third of the fee for another backstreet abortion. He and two friends had shared a girl, and again no-one knew who had actually knocked her up. After this second experience, Derek never touched another woman.

Moving to Paris was quite straightforward; Derek only had to do a couple of translations to get the AFP job. Two weeks later they were on their way back down to Dover in the bomber.

But the calm Channel crossing was in stark contrast to the Paris they came across. It was like heading into civil war. President General de Gaulle was under attack from a rebel general from Algeria. The Parisians were expecting troops to parachute onto the Champs Elysées at any moment. There were tanks on the streets. Both wondered whether leaving England had been the right choice.

But Paris soon won them over. It was, Ennio decided, just as chaotic as Rome, but the people were more polite. They called him *monsieur*, and he couldn't help but be flattered.

He learned French at the Alliance Française and passed the notoriously difficult French driving test at the first attempt. He also got a job straight away, driving around as a messenger boy for a travel agency in a Citroen that rattled passengers to their bones.

With both of them working they were better off than in London, which meant eating out more, mostly in Left Bank student restaurants where the waitresses didn't shave their armpits. Ennio nailed one in a stairwell – it was a bit of a triumph at the time. Over dinner she made faces at him, so he followed her round the back and chased her as she ran upstairs to the storeroom. After he'd had his fill she started talking. As his French was still not good enough to understand her, he just said *au revoir* and walked away.

Within a few months he learnt how to prepare some of the local dishes. *Truite en papillotte* was his specialty. The two lovers rented a classy bed-sit in the 16th *arrondissement* and for a while felt like they were going up in the world.

Around eight months into this new life, Derek fell down the stairs blind-drunk after a night on the town with a mate who had come over from London. He was performing a cabaret act.

The doctor thought it was just bruising, but after two days he rolled up into a ball that wouldn't unroll. His broken rib had punctured a lung.

He was in hospital for a fortnight, and Ennio went in twice a day with fruit and newspapers and a fresh subject of conversation nicely prepared.

The other patients on the ward were impressed by what they called Ennio's 'devotion'. They would compliment Derek. 'What a good friend you have there. You don't realise how good,' they said. When he heard of the compliments, Ennio was surprised. 'That's what friends are for, no?' he said. 'I haven't had many, so I appreciate the ones I do have.'

Derek was in reality the only real friend Ennio had had since childhood. He was the only person who cared whether Ennio lived or died. Many a day he woke up thinking of his upbringing, the humiliations of the kitchen work, the shoe-shining. He was in essence a bum, he concluded. Only Derek, who believed in achieving the impossible, was capable of giving him a morale boost. They fell out frequently, but Ennio's psychological dependency would always drive him back.

They were in Paris for seven years. Ennio thought constantly about breaking free and setting up on his own, but he kept putting it off. Life without Derek seemed too daunting, and in any case he was comfortably off, though not well off enough to support both himself and a French girl. He was free to play the field as far as women were concerned as long as Derek didn't know, which meant sex, nothing else. No relationship. For a while this arrangement worked well.

For their holidays they would travel down to Rome together, sometimes even up to Morrea to see Ennio's mother, but only her; Ennio by this time thought himself to be intellectually superior to the other ignoramuses in the village.

Instead of hanging around in the village bar, they would go down to the dried up river Liri and sunbathe naked, listening to the BBC World Service. Sunbathing naked was one of Derek's favourite pastimes. He liked to get naked in public places – once on the bank of the Seine as barges passed by. On these occasions he would demand Ennio satisfy him.

As always Ennio found the sex sickening but felt he was in no position to refuse. His life, improving a little every month, was based on their relationship. So they lived like a little couple, with Ennio playing the part of the woman, or the whore. Whenever they entered a restaurant, Derek would open the door to let Ennio pass. The same applied to the car door. Derek would open the passenger side before getting in himself. And of course, if Ennio needed anything, they would go shopping together, with Derek picking up the tab.

Later, with Françoise, Ennio would branch out in his own right. Later still, in Vietnam, he would become someone, a man of standing, and by then he was not afraid to drop Derek and concentrate on beautiful women. But that was later. For the first years in Paris, Ennio was the trailing spouse. He could make demands, but he couldn't make good on any threat to break away.

*

One summer they went further afield, to Tangier and Marrakech, towns even poorer than Rome, inhabited by boys even more desperate than the Romans. One night they were sitting on the street sipping gin and tonic when a shoeshine boy scampered up with his box and his brushes. He made his presence felt by banging the brush against the box.

Ennio saw himself. The knocking of the brush against the wooden box was painful to listen to. In the wink of an eye he was forced to re-live every moment of humiliation.

'I'm so grateful for what you have done for me,' he told Derek with a lump in his throat. 'Where would I be if you had not found me that night near the Galeria Colonna?' Derek was embarrassed by the confession. It offended his British stiff upper lip. 'You have helped me too,' he said, uncomfortably. 'Until I met you I was a prisoner inside my own head.'

The heart-to-heart nevertheless made Derek happy. He would later refer to the Moroccan trip as the 'zenith' of his relationship with Ennio.

As with all zeniths, it preceded a fall.

Things began to change when Ennio got a new job – chauffeur for the New Zealand Embassy.

In no time his charm had won over the ambassador and his wife, who invited him out to dinner and gave him cute presents such as handkerchiefs with his initials on them. It was hardly the start of a career, but he started to move in different circles.

Derek meanwhile was promoted. He became the Africa correspondent for Agence France Presse and immediately began jetting around the world. A new chapter opened up.

*

For the Englishman, scoops were gold dust. While he was scouting around Africa looking for them, Ennio had Paris to himself.

The time spent apart created an inevitable wedge. Derek flew back into town to discover things weren't quite the same. They took several days to get used to each other.

Ennio was still expected to play housewife when Derek was around, which he did, initially. One time he played nurse too, during Derek's convalescence from hepatitis contracted in the Congo.

But at the same time, Ennio's new status as a single man opened up possibilities he hadn't previously considered.

To start with, the landlord made passes at him.

They were living in a roomy second floor flat in the 'red' suburb of Suresnes, near the Bois de Boulogne. The landlord, a cripple who walked thanks to a contraption strapped to his boot, lived in the flat downstairs. They gave him the nickname, 'the pig', due to his general unattractiveness and poor hygiene.

Out of boredom and curiosity, or at least that was his explanation to himself, when Derek was jaunting around some exotic location, Ennio let the pig take him out to dinner. They actually went out twice and both times, after the landlord had paid the bill, he gave Ennio a kiss on the cheek and patted his thigh.

Ennio saw no reason not to come clean to Derek about these '*soirées*'. It wasn't as if anything untoward had occurred. But Derek didn't see things the same way.

'Why the hell did you allow it? Why didn't you storm out and tell him to get stuffed?' Derek asked, as if a pat on the thigh were a big deal.

'I didn't feel in a position to say no,' Ennio said. 'He might have thrown us out if I had resisted.'

'You scheming little Roman!' Derek said, all worked up. 'What ambiguous shits you are. Compromise, compromise. Anything to save your skin, isn't it? Any British boy with an ounce of pride would have pissed on his face!' That night they slept in separate beds for the first time while under the same roof.

Ennio's first steps towards independence had been forced on him by Derek's absence, but he soon started to like it. It felt good to decide for himself where to eat, with whom to spend time and with whom to have sex. Ennio then went further; he didn't see why he had to be home for dinner every night just because Derek was back in Paris. Or even to sleep in the same apartment.

The pig was just a warm-up. Things really started to move when he met Françoise.

She was a second secretary at the New Zealand embassy with responsibility for child welfare. France was the world leader in the sphere, she said.

A smallish brunette with long hair which got into her mouth while she talked and breasts which fitted neatly into your hand, she wasn't the most beautiful woman Ennio had met. She was however dynamite in bed and liked 'a bit of rough', an expression Ennio noted in his vocabulary book and which fast became one of his favourites.

The first time he slapped her in bed she was shocked, or at least she pretended to be. But soon afterwards she was asking for it. 'Hit me. Hit me,' she murmured. 'No problem, sweetheart,' Ennio replied.

He started taking his rings off before getting into bed but still found it difficult to whack her around without leaving marks. She took to making up stories in the office to explain her bruises. She claimed on one occasion she had been mugged. When she refused to go to the police her colleagues became suspicious.

The two had become acquainted in the embassy car. Ennio drove her home one night after a champagne party. They knew each other a little already but had never exchanged more than pleasantries. She invited him up for a drink, and soon after they were at it, banging away on the sofa.

As soon as she was on the scene, Derek was banished from Ennio's mind. He started spending all his weekends with Françoise. Within weeks he accepted her offer to move into her apartment.

'That way there will be no sneaking around,' she said, repeating the line Ennio had used with Derek back in Rome.

He decided to come clean. The conversation with Derek was fairly simple.

'I've met someone. A New Zealander.'

'A New Zealander?'

'Yes, I chauffeured her home after an embassy reception. She invited me in. I'm in love with her. I'm sorry for us.'

'What's her name?'

'Françoise.'

'And she's from the Commonwealth with a name like that? When did you meet her?'

'During the Congo.'

After this chat they ceased talking and started communicating via notes. Derek staggered around the flat like a drunkard, unsure how to react. He had been so sure of Ennio's fidelity he was totally at a loss when his creature broke free. It was a pathetic sight. Whenever Ennio entered the room he would stare at him forlornly like a puppy.

From Ennio he got no sympathy. 'That's the way things go,' Ennio surmised. 'The abused become the abusers as soon as they get the chance.'

For a short while he honestly thought he was in love with his New Zealander. For once he could be seen in public with a woman. It felt good. They enjoyed a typical Paris romance, petting in the gardens on every street corner. 'It's true what they say,' he whispered to her in the *Jardins de Luxembourg*. 'Paris really is made for lovers.' She giggled.

But the problems soon broke the surface of their tranquil pool. Françoise was satisfied in bed; it was Ennio's domain. But he quickly found he could not say anything to impress her when clothed.

Derek would leave strangers open-mouthed with stories of the Berlin airlift and the siege of Stanleyville. Ennio on the other hand knew most about washing pans and feeding pigs. He had never claimed to be an intellectual, only pretended to be one. Françoise thought of him as her little poodle, a toy-boy, a good laugh and a hammer in bed. She couldn't take him seriously.

But Ennio would not give up without a fight. Françoise needed impressing, and Ennio knew just the man. It was a big favour to ask, but he was sure he could get away with it.

He at first sent Derek a note saying he would pop around. When he arrived Derek could hardly hide his desperation; it was written all over his face. Ennio softened him up further by cutting his hair. It was a bit of a gay thing to do, he knew – but well, you have to play the part, don't you?

The fringe between forefinger and thumb, he got down to business.

'I want you to make a good impression with Francoise,' he said. 'Could we all go out? You could tell her about the Congo and all those killings and the Berlin airlift. Tell her things that will make a woman shiver.'

Maybe he did it for existentialist kicks. Maybe he would have done anything just for the chance to spend more time with Ennio. Maybe he was a masochist. Whatever the reason, Derek said yes.

The three of them met in the Trocadero in the 16th *arrondissement*, where the wrinkly old ladies went with their shampooed poodles. Ennio made way so that Françoise and Derek were sitting close together. He then withdrew from the conversation and just listened. This would get her juices going, he told himself.

'Ennio's been telling me about your foreign assignments,' she said with a slight New Zealand lilt. 'Is it really as dangerous as it seems to be for us folk back home?'

'Only as dangerous as you imagine it to be,' Derek said, looking her in the eyes. 'If you anticipate peril down the road, you'll probably find it. Imagination can kill.'

'Tell me about Germany,' she said. 'Tell me a story.'

'It's 1949, the time of the Berlin airlift. People fear a third world war at any minute. I'm based near Düsseldorf,' he started. 'By day, I'm sergeant in the education corps. But really I'm a lieutenant in intelligence. We spied on our own men, you see. My job was to eavesdrop, find out how scared they would be if there was an invasion.'

Françoise was already bewitched, her eyes wide-open. It was working already, Ennio thought, she's wetting her pants.

'At night, I worked with a field security station. Our main job was surveillance of defectors from the east in case they double-crossed us. One man did. He was called Otto Van something. He'd somehow got himself a job with the British as a technical translator and pinched some stuff. He was on the run but every so often went to the same bar – one of those big beer halls.'

Derek pointed to his big nose. 'Look at me,' he said. 'As you can see I can easily pass for a German. So I sat unnoticed in that bar for a whole week endlessly nursing beers. People were waiting outside in the freezing cold, counting on me. Then at last Otto appeared.

'He was wearing glasses that weren't his but I recognised him by a mole on his cheek. Big moment now: I stagger to the toilets as if drunk. I lock myself in, stand on the seat, open a small skylight, and wave a red handkerchief out of it. I do a Judas.

'He's at the bar, ordering. I stand next to him, slightly swaying. Then the door opens. My boss, a captain, comes in. He spots me. He saunters towards the target without looking at Otto. Two military police barge in through the main door, two others through another, and the boss touches the defector on the forearm and says: I arrest you on orders of the British Army of the Rhine.'

'What happened to him?' asked Françoise.

'We shot him.'

That night she let Ennio do whatever he wanted. They hardly slept and in the morning she had new bruises over much of her body.

Ennio never asked Derek why he was so obliging with Françoise. In Paris in those days people dared to do the unthinkable. Relationships were fluid. Taboos were being broken all the time. Time and space combined to create an oddly 'Parisian' ambiance which some, Derek and Ennio included, drank in greedily.

The 'countess', an old Rome friend of Derek's, was less understanding when she came to Paris on a social call. She was in Ennio's opinion an ugly snob and a bore. He couldn't figure out why Derek maintained contact with her so diligently. Derek's choice of friends was often puzzling. He seemed to seek out the seedier side of life, the oddballs, the marginalised, the unbalanced. In old age his predilection was for masochistic relationships with young boys who would rip him off.

Ennio made a reservation for four in a chic restaurant in the countess' honour. The moment she saw Françoise she turned up her nose.

'In my days,' the countess told Françoise, 'ladies and gentlemen kept to their station. We did not abdicate our responsibilities. Ennio here is a chauffeur. He wears a peaked cap.'

'So what of it?' said Françoise.

'You, if I am informed correctly, are a diplomat, even though a woman,' the countess said, emphasising her upper class English accent.

'Yes, so what?' said Françoise.

'Slumming a bit aren't we, dear?'

Derek sat there and said nothing, happy within that his ally had come to his aid and wondering whether he would get through the first bottle of wine before lunch degenerated into a fistfight.

Françoise raised her hand a little as if to slap but let it drop. 'That's only out of respect for your age,' she said. The countess smiled.

'Does he hit you?' she asked.

'That's impertinent.'

'Most Italians do, you know.'

'So what if he does?'

'They're very clever, you know. They will at first make you feel like a queen. You are the only woman in the world. They will stop at nothing to please you. They will play and play you, like a fish on a line. And when they have landed you, they will take what you have and run.'

'You seem to know something about it,' said Françoise.

The countess (no-one but Derek knew her real name) started raising her voice so that fellow diners could overhear. She hinted she would tip off a gossip magazine about the 'sordid love affair' between a diplomat and her chauffeur. 'Are you being wise my dear Françoise? Couldn't this liaison damage your career?' she said.

The New Zealander didn't like the topic of conversation. 'I resent this interference. Can we get on with our food? It's in your honour after all.'

The countess patted Françoise's wrist. 'Now don't get upset my poor girl. You've heard of the *Journal de Dimanche*?' Françoise nodded.

'Well then, you know it's a scandal rag. Any tit-bit of smut will do. Just one phone call. I see it already: "Françoise and the Chauffeur – Off For a Spin!" Would your embassy like that?'

'What is this? Who'd make that call? You?' Françoise was also raising her voice now.

'Now don't be silly,' the countess commanded. 'Yours is a world of men. You must be very brilliant to have got where you are. But those men will do all they can to undo it all. One of them may make the call. We have an important journalist with us tonight and he will confirm it.'

Derek inclined his head gravely.

'All right. Point taken. I'll think about it. Now tell me why you still live in Rome if Italians are the selfish brutes you make them out to be?' With this she pulled Ennio towards her by his hand and whispered in his ear. He grinned foolishly.

'You must excuse me, my dear,' said the countess. 'We old ladies develop a very rational frame of mind in the end, you know. We grow careful and cold and ponder before acting. I suppose I was merely wondering rationally what on earth you two can have in common.'

'Hasn't it occurred to you? Haven't you seen? It does happen to people, you know,' Françoise said in her defence. 'What's the matter with you? What is it? Envy? Old age? Spite? I pity you! Can't you see? We're in love!'

Half the restaurant was following by now.

Drawing herself up to her full sitting height and putting on her best look of scorn, the countess threw back her head into a caricature of haughtiness. Her upper lip curled, showing huge front teeth. She let out a terrible, drawn-out nasal snigger. 'Love,' she thundered. 'Love is a disease!'

Whispered translations raced around the dining hall: *'L'amour, c'est une maladie!'*

On the way back to the railway station, Ennio and Françoise sat in the back of the car. There was no conversation. Then from the front the countess and Derek heard rustlings and urgent little moans. Their movements caused the steering wheel to give little tugs. Derek glanced in the rear-view mirror. Françoise was on her back, her head jammed into a corner. Ennio's mouth was clamped over hers. He had her breasts out.

Derek glanced to his right. The countess was looking straight ahead through her lowered veil, erect with petrified outrage. Françoise had won their contest.

Derek's indulgence for Ennio's dallying wore thin after this. He was absent from Paris again, for three months, during which time he plotted his revenge. Upon his return he invited Françoise out for tea, saying he needed to talk to her in private.

Back in the Trocadero, he softened her up with stories of Nigeria.

'The escorts took us to a shed. The body lay on a table inside. It was Chief Okotie Eboh, no mistake. He was in torn and blood-covered robes. He was wearing a wristwatch. They told me to unstrap it. The inscription on the back bore the chief's name in English. What further proof did I need? Then we left the shed for an isolated copse. They pointed to the bole of a tree growing out of a puddle of caked blood, with bits of clothing sticking out of it. They pointed at the bites of an axe against the bark. They'd hacked him to death against the tree. Then they showed me fresh earth at the side of the shallow grave they'd pulled him out of…'

'And what happened next,' asked Françoise, agog.

'I got out of Nigeria pretty fast. I wouldn't be surprised if the country descends into civil war.'

A pause. Then Derek: 'So what happens now?' She knew he was referring to her relationship with Ennio, which had hit a rocky patch.

'Well, there is something between us. I can't let him down just like that after the marvellous times we've had. I'm not sure I want to either.' She giggled.

'In that case, surely it would be better if I faded away. I feel *de trop* you know,' Derek said.

Françoise looked startled. 'No don't do that,' she said. 'You and Ennio have been friends so long. Oh no, don't. I've robbed you a lot of his company, I know, but I also know what value he puts on you. Why should you leave him?'

‘Well to be frank I’m a bit fed up with this sharing business.’

‘What sharing business?’

‘The sharing of Ennio.’

‘But we don’t share him.’

‘We both go to bed with him.’

She looked flustered, then laughed and tapped Derek’s nose with a bit of finger. ‘Don’t be facetious. You’ll have to think of a better excuse than that. You clearly don’t know Ennio. Ennio of all people!’ She smiled to herself, reliving some untellable moment.

‘I do know,’ Derek said.

Françoise snapped back down to earth. ‘What do you know?’ she demanded.

‘I could hardly touch him for your bites on his inner thigh last night.’

‘Last night? What do you mean ‘last night’? He was with me last night,’ she said.

‘Yes, and then it was my turn.’

Françoise jumped up. ‘You’re lying!’

‘You nipped his balls as well. He jumped when I got them in my mouth.’

All around them people were crash-landing cups to follow the sequel.

‘I don’t believe you,’ said Françoise, still standing. There was another pause and then her nose wrinkled with disgust. Her face became contorted as she clutched her throat and began to choke. It looked as if she was about to vomit.

‘You’re trying to destroy us, aren’t you?’ she gasped.

‘No, just seeking clarification, Miss Second Secretary,’ Derek said, a smile breaking out as he watched her stagger towards the street.

The next time he rang the buzzer of what he supposed was his flat, Ennio didn’t get an answer. He kept his finger on it until Françoise picked up. ‘Get lost,’ she said. He buzzed again and asked for an explanation. ‘Go ask your boyfriend you little queer,’ she said.

Ennio rushed straight around to Derek’s place, his old flat, and found him wearing a cricket box. The crockery was stowed away. Derek was carrying a breadboard to fend off a knife attack.

Ennio lunged with outstretched arms, two fists at once. Derek went reeling against the curtained windows.

'You told her on purpose! You bastard!' he screamed.

Gripping the windowsill, Derek kicked hard ahead of another charge and caught Ennio in the knee. It hurt, giving Derek a second to get out of the way. Ennio's punches were lost in the curtain material, but they splintered the windows. Glass fell tinkling onto the steps leading up to the front door.

'She won't let me in!' Ennio yelled with such violence it gave Derek goose-flesh. Ennio fumbled to open a kitchen drawer, looking for a carving knife, but found it locked. Derek seized his wrists from behind and dragged them away. Ennio elbowed Derek in the stomach, screaming again: 'Don't touch me. I'm finished with you!'

Turning around he landed two vicious jabs in Derek's face, knocking him onto the floor tiles. He lay there dazed while Ennio calmly undid his fly and urinated on him, up and down as if he were a flowerbed, kicking at the same time.

Derek came round from his daze and, slowly realising what he had been subjected to, he let off writhing kicks from below. One of them, a fluke, landed square on Ennio's private parts. The Italian howled, bent double, and stumbled back to the couch, bumping into things as he went.

The set-to over, Derek went to have a shower. On his return he found Ennio face down on the bed, sobbing. 'If I lose her, I'll kill you,' he cried into the pillow. He then scrambled to his feet and barged out, wiping his eyes with a forearm. 'You won't see me again,' he said as he crossed the threshold.

When he eventually did get to see Françoise again, she was unmovable. She didn't even mention Derek, but insisted she wanted the relationship to end because Ennio was too violent. 'You go too far with your beatings when we are in bed,' she said.

'It may have got a little out of hand, but you wanted it,' Ennio pleaded.

'A bit out of hand? I had to have an operation after what you did to me. You made me scream in agony. It was frightening. It has all gone too far. Who knows what might happen next? It's my fault too.

I'm older than you, I should have known better.' She added sternly: 'Ennio, that's it. It's over.'

Ennio looked down at his shoes and said nothing.

'But there's one other thing,' Françoise said. 'I've got you a new job.'

After a few nights lodging in a cheap Paris hostel, Ennio was given a ticket to Rome where he was to work for the New Zealand embassy as an Italian-English interpreter for a team that travelled around Italy interviewing prospective immigrants. Françoise made it clear that if he didn't accept she would hand him over to the police.

Two weeks later she wrote a letter to Derek. 'If he wants to come back to Paris, I wouldn't have him if I were you. To myself, I used to call Ennio the bloodsucker. Give me, give me, give me… Little favours. Little loans. Phone call after phone call. So insistent. He wore me out. I may seem a bit of a prickly pear, but all I want is a bit of peace. I see life as a plain with railway lines crossing it, and I need those lines to guide me across. He doesn't. It's one thing today, another tomorrow. Crisis, crisis, crisis. I couldn't stand it any more. He was getting me down. That's why I think you shouldn't let him come back. Otherwise, he'll pull you down as well, drown you.'

The love triangle was scattered. Ennio was based in Rome, where the old obsessions, sport, spaghetti and cars, quickly made him miserable. He was in his mind no longer Italian. 'The Italians stink like corpses,' he complained to his sister. 'They don't even read the newspapers or listen to the radio.'

Françoise stayed in Paris, while Derek was sent for six months to Aden, where British troops were under attack by gunmen clamouring for independence. 'See Aden as a jail,' he wrote in his diary. 'Will be a challenge to my toughness.' And then later: 'It's the intoxication I always feel with him… But I know that whatever happens, the link that will continue to tie me to him is the fear of loneliness, a small, but fundamental cog in me.'

Derek and Ennio were soon writing to each other. Derek at first forwarded Françoise's letter.

Ennio replied: 'She said she wanted to forget me, to suffer no more. I wept like a child. I wanted to run away. I couldn't sleep. I thought I was going mad.'

In a second letter Ennio went on: 'Once she asked what I thought would happen to you. I said I could not imagine – that career was your priority. In any case, I told her, as long as I have a roof over my head, he'll always be able to sleep under it. That took her aback a bit, but now I'm glad I said it.'

And a third: 'I wrote to her that she was a cheap prostitute. I'm going to demand 2,000 francs from her. We will call it a fine. She looks like a peasant, but she'd give her soul for sex. She turns into an animal.'

The letters grew tender. 'Without you, Italy is a graveyard,' Ennio wrote. 'I hope you're not too depressed because I am not with you. I so much want to be with you, but until we find a way out, we must behave like this, like two hermits. What I get so angry about now is the precious time I wasted on her instead of being happy with you.'

And again, drunk this time: 'I'm in a bar now doodling pictures of my monster's face – yours – on the wet bar top. I wonder when I will no longer need to. I wonder when the monster will be beside me, at a bar, say. I hope he won't frighten me! I'll be brave!'

Derek's letters were less emotional, but he couldn't keep the truth from his diary.

'Something has happened,' he wrote. 'I cannot sleep. I don't do my work properly. I am late with stories and couldn't care less. Ennio has not written for six weeks. It's as if I have hurtled down a shaft and am now spread-eagled at the bottom. I cannot trust him with my emotional needs. But what other circuit is there to take the load?'

With still no word from Ennio, another entry: 'I try to imagine reasons. He has met somebody else. He is in hospital after a car accident. Without Ennio, a terrorist is welcome to kill me.'

Ennio re-appeared after two months. He wrote from Sicily. 'I've met a girl called Cettina. She's in love with me but she is stuck with her boyfriend because she doesn't want any trouble, if you know what I mean.' He meant a bullet in his skull, Derek knew.

'Many Sicilian girls marry men they do not want,' Ennio continued. 'So to be on the safe side I have been enjoying the wife of the branch manager of an insurance company. Don't be jealous. Shall we meet in Messina? Do you remember the cathedral? We discovered it together. We had lunch on the pavement in the restaurant facing the bell tower. The golden figures struck the hour with raised hammers, do you remember?'

As soon as the British gave Aden its independence, Derek bought a ticket for Rome. He took the train down to Messina.

Ennio was sunburned. On top of a tightly tailored shirt of extra small check he was wearing a turquoise green suit. 'What do you think to the get-up?' he asked after giving Derek a business-like handshake instead of the usual kiss on both cheeks. He swung around to show off his buttocks through the back vents. 'All I had to do was to tell him how to answer a couple of questions.'

As emigration interviewer he had a powerful position – the chance to change someone's life. 'One old man wanted to go to Australia but would not have stood a chance if I hadn't helped him out, because he had tuberculosis,' Ennio boasted.

The Italian got the better of Derek, who became all righteous. 'How could you?' he protested. 'That's double-crossing people who rely on you.'

'Stop shouting!' said Ennio. 'He's got a berth. I've got a suit. What's wrong with that?'

'If you had your way the entire Mafia would be exported to Australia, wouldn't it?' Derek said. 'Who's going to bribe you next?'

Ennio let off a slap. It connected loudly. Derek went off slouching into a corner while Ennio stared at the boats in the harbour. After a few minutes Derek wandered back over.

'If you think I'm having dinner with you wearing that thing, you can eat alone. I'll get the plane in the morning. *Fini*!' he said.

'All right, all right. Don't get so worked up,' said Ennio, striding back to his hotel to change. Derek followed like a well-trained dog.

In the hotel room, the phone rang. It was Ennio's embassy employer. While his back was turned, Derek looked over his untidy dressing table and saw letters spilling out of his document case, some in Ennio's own hand. Derek skimmed through them.

One, a carbon copy of a sent letter, began: 'My Dear Dear Harold. I did so much enjoy our meetings in Rome. I do hope to become an eternal friend of yours. I feel that our meeting at the flower shop was not chance but fate.'

The reply was written in a crumpled hand and headed Utica, Michigan. 'I am writing to let you know I think of you often and that I am grateful for being with you last Saturday. This feeling is reserved for you as I met no-one on this trip for whom I felt the same. Your very good friend, Harold.'

The phone conversation became protracted, so Derek read another.

'My Dear Harold. It was a great pity we spent so little time together. The next time you are in Rome, I will introduce you to my little flat. It is not in the centre, but quiet and intimate.' The word 'intimate' had been underlined twice.

Ennio was still occupied. The conversation was about re-arranging the order of interviews.

'Why don't you come with me on a trip?' Harold wrote in another letter. 'If we get on OK, perhaps you would be interested in coming to this country. I would sponsor you. Will I be able to have supper with you at your place the next time I'm in Rome?'

'Of course,' Ennio had replied. 'If you come, we will have more than a meal at home. If you want, you can also stay here. I would very much like to come to the US. Actually, if you could sponsor me, it would be too nice and great. To answer your question, yes I like gold.'

'I thought Englishmen did not read other people's letters,' said Ennio, entering the room and snatching them out of Derek's hand.

'Who's the cheap prostitute now? Who the bloody hell is this?'

'Those are carbon copies. I never sent the originals,' Ennio stuttered. 'He's an American. It was while you were in Aden. He was in a flower shop.'

'And what were you doing in a bloody flower shop?' Derek demanded.

'I interpreted for him…'

'And what else did you do for him?'

'Nothing. Nothing. He just took me to two restaurants. They were nice ones though.'

'You mean he took you out twice?'

'I was at a loose end. I had nothing to do.'

'Now you're at a loose end,' said Derek, storming out of the room, down the stairs and out of the hotel

This time it was Ennio who was the dog following its master.

'He was rich,' Ennio shouted after Derek. 'He gave me a hundred dollars for going out with him. That's all.'

Derek walked on without saying anything, down a narrow street towards the cathedral.

'All right, I shouldn't have done it. I was lonely and I admit the money was useful. But there was nothing else.'

Mr Angry gave no answer.

Ennio came to the point. 'You want to know if he touched my prick, don't you?' It was not the kind of conversation the nosy old men and women of Messina were used to over-hearing. Shutters sprung open and men in vests leaned out. People wrapped in sheets appeared on wrought-iron balconies. 'My prick!' Ennio shouted, not caring whom he embarrassed.

'Shut up! *Zitto*!' came furious whispers from above.

Derek turned around and switched on his Oxford University lecture voice.

'I know how you see life,' he said pompously. 'Life is *me* plus help. I like the person who helps *me*. Help equals friendship. You can't tell the difference, can you? Because it's convenient. And how do you say thank you? With your prick and your arse. I mean, what else have you got?'

'Listen, I'm trying to tell you,' Ennio said. 'He didn't touch my prick, and if you don't believe me, you can go right on walking without looking around and I'll never bother you again.'

Derek didn't stop.

'I was lonely. I wish I'd never met him,' Ennio carried on after him. 'You read my letters to Aden, didn't you? I only want you. You know I'm not lying.'

The problem with lying, of course, is that once you've been caught it gets a lot harder to get away with it again.

'But how can I know?' Derek said. 'As soon as the poor baby is lonely, as soon as I'm off somewhere, he lets himself be picked up by the first rich American he sees. He's friendly and you respond like a dog, panting. Who are you? What do you care? And if there's been a first American, why not a second? *Two* hundred dollars! And what's wrong with a third? With *three* hundred dollars! How can I know?'

'You'll know because I'll be with you. From now on, I'll follow you anywhere,' said Ennio.

'What did you say?' Derek turned around, his heart beating faster.

'I'll follow you anywhere.' Ennio lifted his arms operatically into the air. His brown eyes were primed but he was not smiling. Derek knew it was for real. 'I'll follow you anywhere,' he repeated.

Flattered by the simplicity of the pledge and the power of its humility, Derek followed it up with an invitation. 'Why don't you come to Tel Aviv for Christmas then?'

Beaming now, Ennio did a little pirouette. They went off to a bar to celebrate their reconciliation.

Halfway through their first bottle of foul white wine, Derek realised something was still rankling.

'I want to get even with your American. I've got to feel better about it,' he said.

'How?' Ennio asked.

'Write him a letter, saying you've had an accident and could he send you a hundred dollars to help pay the hospital bill.'

'What would the point be?' said Ennio.

'If he sends it, you'll give half to me. We'll be in it together.'

Ennio gave Derek his hand to shake on the deal, uncertainly. They drafted the letter there and then. Derek insisted on adding a few grammar mistakes to give it authenticity. 'The baddest accident you will imagine,' the letter read. 'A wound to my leg. One hundred of dollars.' Ennio signed it. Derek sealed it and gave it to the concierge to send the next day.

*

In Israel, on holiday, Ennio learnt to take photographs and sold a few to Agence France Presse. But it was in Vietnam that he made his mark, that he became a professional… that he found fame.

The chance came about because the AFP man in Indochina had been expelled for interviewing North Vietnamese officers in the captured northern city of Hue. He had been bundled off to Bangkok, and AFP wanted someone in Vietnam as quickly as possible.

Derek told Ennio the good news on the telephone in January 1968. Ennio resigned his Italian job the next day. His self-confidence was at an all time high. There was no way he was going to miss this adventure. He told himself: 'I am about to become a freelance photographer!' The boy from the backward village who counted down the days before seeing his mother was set for the big time, for the adventure of his life. Boredom was banished, and only years later, when back in Rome, would he count the days going by again.

He immediately researched what to wear in Saigon. Given the temperature, there was no point going with his leather jacket. So when he got off the plane he had a short-sleeve shirt, some cotton trousers, and a small suitcase.

Getting to Vietnam via Bangkok was chaotic. Derek didn't know exactly when he would arrive, so there was no welcome party. Ennio phoned the AFP office when he got in, sleepy and unshaven, and hung around the flocks of meaty looking Marines while Derek drove to the airport. The camera and kit weighed almost as much as his suitcase.

'So you see. We've made it,' Ennio said, pecking each of Derek's cheeks twice as he had learnt to do in Paris.

'I'll show you something tonight,' Derek said. Ennio presumed he was referring to nightlife, though this was puzzling as a 7pm curfew was in place throughout the city.

They went to the flat they would be sharing. It had a big terrace and looked as if it had been built room by room, a year at a time, a bit like some of the houses you see in the suburbs of Rome.

Skinny old Monsieur Cuc, the landlord, came out with his family to say hello. He lived in the apartment below and looked unwashed in his singlet. He was quite polite, bowing so low he could touch the ground and smiling broadly when he stood back up, showing packed rows of crooked teeth.

His ugliness was more than made up for by his daughter, Madmoiselle Cuc, who said she was 17 and who had put her silk *ao dai* on to greet the foreigners. As she giggled, covering her mouth, Ennio began to think of a strategy for giving her a roll, but thought better of it considering that she lived on the doorstep.

There was about an hour to kill before curfew, so they took a stroll downtown. Saigon did not fit in with the image Ennio had of the Far East. There were foreign expats everywhere, and once out of the nasty area where the flat was located there were residential neighbourhoods with tree-lined streets. This could have been Paris, the 16th *arrondissement*.

Only closer to the centre were there signs of the army. Huge black power lines hanging like spaghetti between lampposts.

Between the posts there were also dark tunnels leading to seedy bars where small girls sat in even smaller mini-skirts on high stools in front of zinc bar-tops. These places smelt of drains.

The only truly impressive building was the town hall, which looked like a wedding cake, a miniature version of that ugly monument at the end of the Fori Imperiali in Rome. There was only one skyscraper at that time, the Caravelle hotel.

They went up in the hotel lift. When he emerged on the flat roof Ennio finally understood what Derek had meant when he said he had something to show.

A party was taking place. Posh Vietnamese women, the city's high society, wearing dresses and high heels, were attending what had become a regular evening spectacle – an outbreak of fighting in the suburbs.

This was shortly after the Tet offensive, the event that turned the Americans into scared jelly. Tet was over but the Vietcong were still attacking Saigon's Chinese quarter, Cholon. They called it 'mini-Tet.'

Cholon was a few kilometres away, so the Vietnamese women felt safe enough to go to the roof and admire the action, giggling and gasping. There were little jumps of fright every time an American plane came in to bomb. 'Oooh, aaah,' they went as a plane strafed Vietcong holed up in a warehouse. One, a twin-engine Dakota known as Puff the Magic Dragon, made them laugh the loudest. When it let off its high velocity guns the sound it made was similar to farting.

The target area was constantly covered in flares. Fires were springing up randomly. Tracer rounds described a graceful parabola of yellow hyphens against the sky and then languidly cascaded upon the Vietcong. It was as if they were being urinated upon.

The women and their suited, shaved husbands were disappointed when they had to leave their show due to the curfew. They went back down in the lifts, back to the chauffeured cars waiting to take them to their villas.

That was just the aperitif. The next day Derek and Ennio went out to see for themselves.

Three of them set off in the direction of Cholon early in the morning in Derek's canvass-topped Deux-Chevaux, an office car with windows like the wings of a frightened hen.

Before leaving they had picked up Oriana Fallaci, the Italian journalist as famous for her outbursts of screaming as for her articles. A small, elf-like woman who was already a household name back home, she had broken up a press conference only the day before when she found her new press card bore the letters *TCN* – Third Country National. 'You insult me! You insult Italy!' she screamed at a petrified American major. 'I am not a TCN. You are a TCN. Italy is not a third country. Italy is a first country. America is number ten!'

'Ma'am,' the major said. 'Please be calm. We'll solve your problem.'

'I've no problem,' she carried on screaming. 'You have big ones! Where is your Renaissance? Where is your Michelangelo, your Dante? My country is not a third one.'

They gave her another press pass that left the 'nationality' panel blank.

It was Derek's idea to take her along. He was attracted to her – in a professional way – because he secretly desired to become famous himself. She had interviewed the likes of Fidel Castro, and Derek wanted to know what made her tick. According to one story, she had had the balls to tick off Castro for his bad body odour.

In the car, she began polite enquiries of Ennio. 'From Abruzzo?' she asked. 'Were you born on a mountain?'

Very quickly their attention turned to the road. It was a Saturday morning, but all the petrol stations were closed. And there were no children running about either.

‘What’s the matter?’ Ennio asked Derek.

‘Nothing that I can see,’ he said. *La Fallaci* stared at him, worried.

As the Citroen chugged forward, the road became more and more deserted. Within minutes there was no longer any sign of the Honda motorbikes and Lambretta vans that normally cluttered roads everywhere.

‘Is this where the Vietcong executed those four journalists the other day?’ Oriana asked. Five newsmen in search of a story had investigated a side-alley when Vietcong had appeared from behind oil drums firing at them with rifles. Four were wounded. The leader of the Vietcong approached and finished them off one by one with his pistol. Unwounded, a 21-year-old Australian played dead until the weapon went ‘click’ for empty. He had told his tale before a hushed press corps.

‘No. We’re nowhere near. It was further on,’ said Derek.

‘There’s no traffic coming the other way!’ Ennio yelled out. ‘Let me out.’

‘Don’t be crazy, there’s nothing to worry about,’ said Derek.

Taking it that reassurance implied the opposite, Ennio yelled out more loudly still: ‘I’m getting out!’

‘You’re not!’ said Derek, accelerating to keep him in. ‘They can see the press stickers. We’re plastered with them…’

‘What do you mean “they”?’ came the voice from behind.

The boulevard had become as clear as a runway and theirs was the only vehicle on it. Against the midday haze, Ennio saw the silhouette of a figure slip across a roof in front of them.

‘Stop, let me get out!’ he pleaded.

‘Sorry! No pissing in the street!’ Derek said.

‘I’ll piss in your face again if you don’t turn around,’ Ennio told him.

Derek slowed down as they went through what was normally a crowded residential area of Cholon. The only people they saw were standing in gaps between buildings.

‘They’re hiding from something!’ Oriana shrieked. ‘Your cousin is right. Please turn back. Please!’ She slithered down from her front seat onto the floor until her head was below the petrol gauge. Stray strands had broken away from her pigtail.

'But it is always like this near a combat zone,' Derek said.

'I don't want to be in combat! I want to go back to Rome!' wailed Ennio from behind. He too had hit the floor.

Derek said he wanted to head for a nearby tank to ask an officer what was going on. And then the car shook to a halt. Oriana had taken the key out of the ignition.

'You're only getting this back if you promise to turn around now and at this precise point, at this very moment, right now,' she said.

'Take a look. There's a tank not far away. We could find out...' Derek warbled.

'Now!' she screamed.

'Have it your own fucking way then. What a story we'd have got. Shit!' Derek snarled, and that was the end of Ennio's first war outing.

They drove back in silence, slowly. Derek drove slowly because he had heard snipers could not resist getaway cars.

Ennio immediately regretted his cowardice. His shame was all the more acute because he had broken down in front of *La Fallaci*. Back at the hotel bar, he downed red wine, head in hands.

'I was a coward, I let you down,' he admitted.

'You said it,' said Derek.

'And in front of her.'

'She didn't do much better...'

'In front of *La Fallaci*! Oh my God! You're ashamed of me. I can tell.'

'Do you really want to go back to Rome, already?'

'No, no,' Ennio protested. 'I didn't mean it. I don't know why I said it.' Then something occurred to him. 'Why? You don't want me to go back, do you?'

La Fallaci came in. She was embarrassed too, covering her eyes with her arm.

'What are you grinning at?' she asked Derek. 'You've forgiven us already?'

'Not quite,' he said. 'But I have been thinking of those five journalists. Had they had someone shouting at them to turn back like you two did, perhaps they'd still be alive. Perhaps you saved our skins.'

‘He’s forgiven us,’ she told Ennio.

‘He might say that but he won’t forget Cholon,’ Ennio said.

‘You seem to know him,’ she said. ‘How long has it been Ennio?’

The ‘cousin’ story had been Derek’s idea. She had her faults, but *La Fallaci* to her credit was not judgmental.

The next day they returned, and Ennio saw action for the first time.

In the afternoon, after the monsoon shower, they drove back past the point where they had turned around, without Oriana this time, and on into the maze of muddy alleys that was Cholon, made of row upon row of cheap building slabs.

They were with US Rangers, an elite force, who were sitting on doorsteps smoking while a lone tank prepared to ‘test’ a block of flats for Vietcong tenants. It let off a single round that shattered windows. After waiting for the dust to clear and some wireless talk, the tank gave the brickwork another blow. Nobody fired back. Thus, concluding nobody was at home, the Rangers stood up and swung on their backpacks to move on.

No sooner had Derek said ‘we’re wasting our time here’ than they were all on the ground with their heads in puddles. The Vietcong were firing from the apartments on automatic from less than sixty metres away. From somewhere further off, a machine-gun opened up. It made a sound like cardboard being torn into strips. The ground beneath the mud started shuddering as though barrels of beer were being dropped onto the pavement.

‘Those are B40s,’ yelled Derek: lethal rocket-propelled grenades, fired from the shoulder from what looked like broomsticks.

Next to them, a Ranger was lying with his cheek in the mud as if sleeping off a heavy night out. Blood was dribbling from his mouth. Ennio thought of his mother, wondering how she would react to the news of his death.

After what seemed an eternity but was in reality two minutes, a lull in the shooting allowed them to get up. They dashed to the nearest doorway and, from there, from doorway to doorway until they made the end of the street. As they approached the Citroen they saw an overturned pedicab with its free wheel still spinning and squeaking. The pedaller lay on his back in the middle of the road. With the fighting still close behind them, Ennio got out his camera and started snapping.

He sold the pedicab shot for fifteen dollars to Associated Press. It was his first sale in Vietnam and the start of a career that would take him higher than any boy from the Abruzzo mountain range could ever dream of.

*

In Vietnam Ennio learned to skydive with South Vietnam's Airborne Regiment. Derek tried to warn him off the idea. 'You could break a leg, or your spine,' he said.

But by this time Ennio was fearless. He knew nothing would happen to him, that he would survive the war unharmed.

'As long as you give at the knees when you hit the ground, you're fine,' he told Derek. 'And it's good exercise.' When he was not reporting to the airbase before dawn, he could be found in the gym keeping his body toned.

Trainee jumpers leapt from a tower attached to a wire. It was forbidden to look at the ground rushing up – instructors were very firm on this point. Those who looked failed the course and didn't get their wings.

Ennio passed at his first attempt. He celebrated in the flat with a bottle of Moet et Chandon. Even Monsieur Cuc's daughter came up to have a glass and listen to some jazz. She was too well behaved for Ennio; she wouldn't even dance. And in any case, from the day he wore his wings and his camouflage combat uniform, Ennio noticed there was no lack of interest on the part of the local girls. He took to wearing his kit everywhere.

As for the work – there was action, but hanging around was more common at first. Waiting on hilltops for helicopters that never came became part of the job, as did lying on one's stomach in the woods waiting for a skirmish to finish.

With a few notable exceptions, the journalist and his snapper usually arrived shortly after the action finished, just like the police. The soldiers they met were constantly on edge, always looking around while they talked. Initially, nothing much happened, but Ennio soon learnt to take advantage of the 'non-stories'.

The attack on the Ashau Valley was a case in point. The valley was supposedly the bottleneck on the Ho Chi Minh trail used by the North Vietnamese to move supplies south. The Americans claimed it was a 'larder'. There were said to be huge amounts of food and ammunition stashed away.

Derek and Ennio went in after a nervous, sleepless night, with the third wave on a Chinook. They soon saw something odd was going on. When they arrived, there was no fighting.

The general in charge said he felt like 'a million dollars' because his men had taken only light casualties. The reality was rather different. The larder was never discovered. The North Vietnamese had given their enemies the slip.

Ennio took photos all the same; of the general looking smug; a bandaged soldier next to a downed Chinook; a GI heating his rations with a candle; the trail itself seen through a machine-gun sight. They all sold. It quickly became a good place to be a photographer. Within a short space of time there was a great deal of demand. Almost everything he took sold somewhere. After his first series of sales he made contact with a variety of agencies, newspapers and magazines, in both Europe and the US.

As the money came in his confidence soared, as did his re-found desire for independence. Why did he need to live in Derek's shadow? The war had turned him into a man, so why walk around hand-in-hand like two schoolgirls? Derek was still calling Ennio by the affectionate nickname *Cocco*, a throwback to their Paris days. It got on Ennio's nerves.

The first solo trips he made were purely social. He went to see the *montagnards*, indigenous hill-folk he had met on a press tour with the Highland commander of the US Fourth Infantry Division. The *montagnards* didn't speak Vietnamese and had oddly-shaped faces, a bit like nuts. The women smoked little clay pipes. Before the war the men were elephant drivers; they bullied the animals into moving logs. They weren't interested in fighting and were on nobody's side, so as a result both sides went after them.

The Americans kept them in an enclosure so as to 'protect them from the Vietcong' and fed and clothed them in the hope that they would give away Vietcong positions, if they found any. They were even given Vietnamese TV, which they couldn't understand, though they enjoyed laughing at the pictures.

La Fallaci was on the same press trip as Ennio. In her no-nonsense style she called the *montagnards* 'prisoners'. The American guides called them 'allies'.

As there were no elephants to drive, they made crossbows out of saplings to sell to the visitors. With the money they bought canned milk. They loved the stuff.

Ennio returned often to see the *montagnards*. He sympathised. They were outsiders like him, and they didn't care who you were as long as you were ready to laugh. 'Their enclosure is like a bubble,' he explained to Derek. 'They are all outcasts. They reminded me of the hopeless, ignorant villagers in Morrea – swept up in the storm of life with no idea what was happening in the next city. The only difference is here they don't have the same obsession with money as everybody does in Italy.'

The *montagnards* accepted Ennio and didn't want him to leave. He chronicled their daily lives in photos. After a few weeks he even thought he understood what they were saying. Most of the time however they all played together like monkeys, throwing things around. 'It's so peaceful there,' Ennio told anyone who would listen. 'The women just sit around drinking canned milk, talking to relatives and laughing all day. I love those people.'

They invited Ennio to an initiation ceremony. He had to drink foul-tasting broth, after which he was given a copper bracelet. He kept the bracelet for the rest of his life.

*

By this time, few in the Vietnam press corps believed the Americans had any chance of a 'formal' military victory. The Vietcong were operating so close to the capital they began shooting their Soviet-made rockets into the city centre.

A big rocket attack woke Ennio and Derek one night. At first they thought it was a hurricane; the blasts ripped the slats from the shutters leaving holes through which you could see the moon. The apartment in which they were sleeping teetered as if made of paper. The flashes seemed to be coming from about twenty metres away. Was this it? Ennio thought. Did the next rocket have his name on it?

But no last-minute life replay ran through his mind. Inexplicably, he knew he wouldn't die that night. He felt destined for other things.

Derek wasn't so sure. He grabbed Ennio as if they had only moments left together. Unlike Ennio, Derek was convinced he would get killed or at least wounded in Vietnam. He bought a flat in Rome for post-injury recuperation, though he too emerged from the war without a scratch, at least physically.

Fifty people died that night and one hundred and fifty were injured. It was one of the heaviest bombardments of the Saigon War. The next morning there was a traffic jam on the road to the coast as people fled the city for the first time. For the Vietnamese, Saigon had become the gateway to hell, but for Ennio the good times were just starting to roll.

By the time General Westmoreland was sacked for failing to win the war, all the top publications knew his name and many, including *Time* magazine, were demanding he work with them. Vietnam was the top story and money rained down.

He was by this time on first-name terms with the entire press corps, thanks both to his reputation and his fluent English and French. He was also having a great time. He would make fun of the generals for the amusement of his colleagues. 'We are a formidable force and time is on our side,' said 'Westy' Westmoreland at one press conference, a cliché he often used. Behind the General's back, Ennio tapped at his wristwatch and then pointed boastfully at his own chest, giving the thumbs-up sign. There were loud guffaws among the hacks. The General, surprised, looked behind him for the cause, only to find Ennio looking as innocent as the day he was born, studying his viewfinder.

Ennio and his parachute get-up became a popular, familiar sight on the streets of Saigon. He relished exploring the city, delighted at how well things were turning out. He loved the Vietnamese and would sit with them for hours on their tiny stools on the pavement, downing noodles and grinning.

He was by this time patrolling – unaccompanied – with the troops, wading through rice paddies in the Mekong Delta. He brought back some of the first shots of Vietcong shrivelled alive by American napalm, as well as deserted American outposts after a Vietcong night attack. The images had a big impact in the US.

The worse things got for the Americans, the better they got for Ennio. When the generals boasted the enemy body count was so high their morale would soon be broken, Ennio sent pictures of Vietcong victories. He wasn't deliberately out to make the Americans look like liars. Indeed, he appreciated the Americans, thought of them as his protectors. But more than this, he had become a businessman, and his pictures told their own story.

Deep down, he knew Saigon wasn't going to top the news forever. President Johnson was already talking about 'an honourable peace'. Soon after General Creighton Abrams replaced Westmoreland, the Americans scaled back operations so that they were going out in only small units, platoons or squads, instead of regiments or battalions.

'What's this small-unit stuff everybody's talking about?' Ennio asked Derek.

'He's apparently keen on small night-ambushes,' said Derek.

'But how am I supposed to shoot ambushes?'

'Get ambushed, I suppose.'

Ennio decided to milk the good times for all they were worth. He was, after all Italian, good-looking, young, finally fearless and a famous war photographer to boot. The women couldn't keep their hands off him.

His first targets were the upper-class local girls who frequented the best hotels. His strategy was simple. He turned up at a hotel to sunbathe and have a cocktail, ignoring the girls completely. This really riled them. The girls, several under the impression they were the equivalent of royalty, were used to being waited on by the rest of Vietnamese society. They got so desperately angry at Ennio's standoffishness they would walk right up to him and introduce themselves. He didn't even have to work for it.

After the first contact was made, the girls would often pretend to play hard to get, but this normally lasted one date only. 'All you have to do is buy them dinner, and then you can do what you want,' he boasted to a friend. 'A few drinks at a party and they're wobbling around and begging you to take them away, to take them anywhere.'

Derek was cramping his style, Ennio decided. He was fed up with Derek's obsession with young men, an obsession that intruded upon their cohabitation. One night, Derek invited a young Vietnamese soldier for dinner. While the soldier was taking a piss in the bathroom, Derek went out to the balcony to stare at him through the bathroom window, standing on a stool. For Ennio, this was too much.

'*Checca!'* he screamed. 'You're nothing more than a *checca*. Why should I live with a *checca?* Tell me! Why?' Checca was a scornful Italian word for gay. Ennio had never used it before. It was the first time he had sexually differentiated between them.

'So what does that make you?' said Derek, furiously stepping down from the stool. 'Just a hypocrite! Why are you living with me then? You're just a whore, a schemer. You give it up because you think it's going to get you somewhere, and when you get there you pretend to yourself that you've never had to compromise. Do you think no-one knows what you're like? Do you think anyone respects you?'

'What did you call me?' said Ennio, clearly shocked.

'A schemer! A whore! A hypocrite!' Derek went on. 'Go on, tell me! Why do you live with a *checca*? What are you doing here?'

Ennio stared at Derek with dilated eyes in disbelief. 'I would never have believed it,' he said. 'I don't know how you can say such things. After all the time we've been together. I can't believe it.' He walked out.

Derek's words hurt because they were true. When Ennio left the apartment he was a war photographer who did as he pleased and who would work only with the best. But back home in bed he still bent over like the girls he used to hang out with near Termini railway station. Most days he would push this unpleasant reality to the back of his mind, but that night Derek brought it out into the open. The truth was too inconvenient. When Ennio met a girl he always came up with an excuse for not going back to their flat. 'There's a rocket hole in the wall,' was a common one.

Derek and Ennio fell out on a personal level that night. They then fell out professionally as well.

Despite the madness and evilness of the war, or perhaps because of it, Derek believed in acting according to a moral code. Around him there was unchecked carnage, rape, corruption and despair, but according to his standards, all reporters and photographers were still expected to act 'responsibly'. Derek believed in right and wrong; it was part of a British superiority complex dating back to the Second World War.

So when Ennio stole photos from Derek's drawer and sold them to Newsweek magazine, Derek flared up like a monster with a bad tooth.

The snaps were of the exhumation following the Tam Ky massacre. Derek had taken them himself. They showed a carrier dragging a macabre harvest of corpses across open ground. They were thought to be too disgusting to use, so Derek put them in a drawer and forgot about them. He then saw them again, while flying to Europe, plastered over the *Newsweek* centrefold, with Ennio's name next to them.

Ennio then crossed the line a second time. A German planter showed him around a plantation near Ban Me Thuot in the Highlands. He took pictures of what turned out to be a Vietcong enclave. The Vietcong found out and put pressure on the German, saying they needed to see the pictures to make sure they gave nothing away. A messenger was sent to Saigon. He came crashing into the AFP office looking for Ennio. The planter's life, the messenger said, depended on the photos.

The AFP journalists told the messenger where to find Ennio – in a fashionable café. Ennio swore he would book onto an American light plane for the Highlands the next morning.

He did nothing.

A good friend of Ennio's, a French correspondent named Alain Saint-Paul, offered to deliver the pictures himself as he was headed for Ban Me Thout on a job. Ennio promised to hand them over but forgot as soon as he met a slim bronzed girl in the Cercle Sportif, a French colonial sports club he had identified as one of the best locations for talent spotting.

'You're an irresponsible shit!' Derek yelled at him when he found out. 'Do you realize what the Vietcong might do to that planter now? His life was in your hands and you did fuck all about it!'

'What do you care? You never met the man. You don't even know his name!' Ennio replied.

'What does his name matter?' said Derek, furious. 'Don't you care at all? Don't you realize the man might be dead already? What sort of person are you? I don't understand you.'

'Why should I care?' said Ennio. 'He offered to show me around. He knew what he was doing. And what about the pictures? Do you think that if I'd let him have them, I'd ever get them back? Besides, *Time* magazine wants them now, not tomorrow.'

Derek was on the verge of punching him. 'You look down on Italy but you're more Italian than the lot of them. That's exactly how they think. "So what? What's it to you? *Che ti frega*? Why should I care? It's nothing to do with me… Why should I bother?" All the time. You disgust me.'

AFP enquired, but people in Ban Me Thuot claimed never to have heard of the German planter. Ennio did not play the guilt game. Maybe they killed him, maybe he just ran away. Who knows? No-one knows. He definitely wasn't taking lessons in morality from an Englishman. Look at all the damage they have done around the world.

Ennio considered himself by this time to be Derek's equal in every way. He was known in his own right throughout the expat community, and attended all the best parties on his own.

With the latest camera equipment, the most fashionable clothes and a Rolex watch that never left his wrist, he spent money as if there were no tomorrow and even then couldn't make much of a dent into his earnings. He often thought back to the days when he was so poor he had to steal from the church. After his upbringing, being rich was easy. He deserved it, he reckoned.

Considering that their relationship was about to become a train wreck, Derek's call back to Paris came at the right time. They were just about on speaking terms for the farewell party. Ennio had decided to stay in Saigon indefinitely. As a peace offering, he agreed to take care of the music, borrowing a tape deck from one of his girlfriends. Two waiters from the Continental Hotel were brought in to serve drinks. He turned up drunk, wearing dark glasses and trousers flown in from Hong Kong. When Miss Cuc made an appearance he asked her to dance, surreptitiously feeling her backside as they swayed demurely.

At around midnight someone announced rockets were falling in one of the suburbs. The American hacks, still within their deadlines, sauntered off, complaining. But the Europeans and locals kept on partying until the sky grew bilious and they were so drunk they could hardly remember who they were.

Derek, in what he thought would be his parting *piece de resistance*, began a striptease at 5am, gamely throwing his garments one at a time over the parapet. When the show got to the critical stage, Ennio rushed up and smothered him with a coat out of rustic prudery.

Annoyed at the interruption to his finale and determined, in his drunken haze, to punish Ennio's desertion, Derek grabbed him and shoved him towards the parapet and the three-storey drop. 'Now you're going to be really airborne!' he shouted. He might have achieved his goal if he had not been detained by the few partygoers still standing.

*

All the AFP staff went to the airport to see Derek off with champagne. His tears showed he thought his departure would be definitive, and the shellshock he suffered back in 'quiet, boring' Paris proved the extent to which the war had got to him. Many of the Saigon-based journalists suffered from inexplicable weeping fits when they got home.

He was, however, gone for only a few months, as his employers wanted him back in the thick of it. So, soon there was another party in his honour, a 'welcome back' dinner party this time.

Ennio attended, but his attention was divided. He filled Derek's glass, but absently, as though he were some ghostly stand-in for someone else. On the one hand he was content to see his former mentor back, on the other he thought the natural break was a good excuse to establish some distance, even to move on to a just-good-friends relationship. During Derek's absence he had been standing on his own two feet for the first time. He was determined not to go back to the lie they lived before.

While Derek was away, Ennio had become close to Alain Saint-Paul. He appreciated the Frenchman's happy-go-lucky, almost Italian, view on life. Even under fire, Alain was always smiling. He trusted more in God than in his flak jacket.

Ennio sought out Alain at the office. They went out to dinner, and off on assignments together. When in Saigon, they met every morning for coffee. There was no touching between them, no outward show of affection except the odd cat-like smile. All the foreign correspondents recognised the affinity between the calm, softly spoken Alain and the emotional Italian who could still raise his voice over some trifling detail. When Alain held up his hand as if to say 'enough' Ennio fell silent.

But this friendship was not to be.

A month after Derek's return, the office phone rang. The friendly voice belonged to Major David, the American spokesman.

'I'm afraid I've got some very bad news for you,' he said. Alain Saint-Paul had been killed. Apparently he was not wearing a flak-jacket. He was out covering Volcano Hill, a Special Forces outpost in the central highlands under siege by the North Vietnamese.

Alain died just as fighting quietened down everywhere else. It was 1969, and despite the Tet offensive Saigon was back in control of the whole countryside. In Hanoi they were warning the people to expect a war of attrition. Nixon had even brought 100,000 troops home.

Four colleagues, a nervous Ennio and Derek included, had to identify Alain's corpse in the American military morgue at Tan Son Nhut airbase.

The fierce air conditioning in the huge white-tiled barn had them trembling so violently they marched quickly behind an orderly down the middle of a long 'dormitory'. None of them dared even glance at the beds of stone on either side of them, all occupied. The orderly halted in a corner of the barn. He folded back a white plastic sheet and there was Alain, smiling as always. His lips were parted as if he had half-understood some joke. His cheeks were rosy, his sandy hair in order and he bore not a scratch. The correspondents looked inquiringly at the orderly.

'The fragment that got your friend was no bigger than an air-gun pellet. It would never have got through a flak jacket,' he said.

The orderly covered up Alain's face and they made for the exit. Upset, they forgot to avert their eyes. The 'beds' were sloping and grooved. Most of their occupants were black; the blacks took the brunt of the fighting. Other orderlies were bent over the bodies in white plastic butcher's aprons. They were working over chests with implements, trying to free identification tags.

Outside, the sudden heat was a punch in the stomach. Ennio was copiously sick.

For days after he was inconsolable. 'Why did it happen to Alain?' he repeated time and again. 'What had he done wrong? Why do they go for nice people? Why hasn't it happened to me?'

Derek offered his shoulder for Ennio cry on. They hugged and decided to move back in together. They chose a flat in the centre of the city.

*

Nixon's disastrous decision to invade Cambodia was the making of Ennio's career. In his memoirs, Derek called it 'one of the most murderous decisions of the twentieth century'.

Derek wrote: 'The trigger for the invasion was the overthrow of the Cambodian ruler, Prince Norodom Sihanouk, saxophonist, film-maker, Master of the Royal Ballet, astute master of compromise. For years he had carefully turned a blind eye towards so-called sanctuaries close to Cambodia's border with Vietnam, used by the North Vietnamese for stocking up supplies or attacking South Vietnam from close quarters. With the Prince out of the way, defenestrated by his own parliament, Mr Nixon saw the chance to neutralise the sanctuaries and thus lessen – as he cunningly explained it to Americans – the threat to American troops during their gradual pull-out.'

After much pestering, the reluctant Americans agreed to take the press into Cambodia. The choppers went in low over a light swell of wooded country. Ennio and Derek were in the same chopper for once.

Supremely confident and still wearing his airborne uniform, Ennio acted with dash and decision as soon as they were put down in a French rubber plantation. Through a regiment of trees, he saw a column of tanks. He jumped out before the skids touched the earth, sprinted up to the tanks as if to beat the four-minute mile, shot off a whole spool in seconds, and began racing back through the disembarking reporters to the chopper they had arrived on, now idling. He was aboard before the rotors were spinning again. Within no time, he was back in Saigon with the first pictures of the invasion.

Communist forces, aware of the US plan, had, meanwhile, decamped further into Cambodia, turning the country into what Henry Kissinger would call a 'single armed camp' which would become 'an overwhelming, insurmountable, and decisive menace to the survival of South Vietnam'.

Ennio went back the next day to immortalise the razing of Cambodia. He took shots of stoned troops slithering down from tanks to loot Snoul, of troops pissing on the still hot ashes, laughing at all the steam they made.

These pictures projected Ennio to the forefront of photojournalism and made him even more money.

In the eyes of his colleagues he had begun to attract an aura. It was as if he were pre-destined to be in the right place at the right time. When he miraculously escaped imprisonment near Phnom Penh, this aura began to take on shades of invincibility. He had become one of the best-known photographers of the war.

When Ennio walked up the driveway of the Phnom hotel, he was trembling so violently Derek hardly recognised him. Derek, who had presumed him dead, was so happy he was lost for words. With tears in his eyes he flung his arms around Ennio, but then stood back, choking – Ennio stank to high heaven. Only a few tufts of hair were sticking up from his skull.

Sitting around the hotel pool, braving the stench, it took the scribes a long time to extract the entire story.

'What kept you going?' one asked.

'I went over and over and over and over Cavaradossi's aria in *Tosca*,' Ennio said.

‘What area?’

‘Where the hell’s Tosca? What highway is that on?’

When they finally understood, one of them shouted out: ‘Sing it for us, Ennio.’ He began. He tried but only a gargling noise came out of his throat. He worked down a whisky but still only painful rasping issued forth. He attempted to start up again and again until his eyes filled with tears and he flopped into a deck chair. The correspondents stood around it, slapping his shoulder from a safe distance.

‘Do you know what I thought of in that hut?’ he croaked so that only Derek could hear. ‘That when I get out of all this, I’ll spend my savings on that little farm for my mother, perhaps in Umbria. She’d love it. I’ve been dreaming of it.’ His other plan he kept to himself.

After his hospital sojourn the two split up again. Derek stayed in Cambodia while Ennio returned to Saigon for rest and recuperation.

Back in Vietnam, unknown to Derek, he got married.

He met Michelle, the daughter of a Vietnamese colonel, at a press conference. She was there to watch her father hold court. As usual Ennio made fun of the colonel behind his back with little hand gestures for the benefit of his colleagues.

His daughter thought this amusing. Afterwards, they got chatting. ‘I like your goatee beard,’ were her first words – it was part of Ennio’s new image. Within six weeks they were married in the Italian consulate in Saigon.

Michelle had long black hair and was a real doll, as the Americans would say; half-French, half-Vietnamese, slim, a perfect oval face and dark almond-shaped eyes that were more open than a typical Vietnamese woman’s. She also had something of the gypsy to her.

She was in fact so beautiful that she would drive waitresses mad with jealousy whenever the couple entered a restaurant. They would look her up and down as if she were a dirty piece of meat before smiling and flirting with Ennio just to see if they could get under Michelle’s skin.

Suddenly, none of Ennio’s friends were interested in seeing him any more unless he was in Michelle’s company. ‘Where is she?’ they would ask if he turned up without her. One or two would even hit on her shamelessly, in front of Ennio. About this he was calm. It made him laugh to think they thought they had a chance.

They didn't have a chance, he knew, because Michelle was a decent woman, not a whore, or at least that is what he thought when he first met her.

She wouldn't even let him kiss her until the fifth date. On their first, in a café immediately after the press conference, he tried for a goodbye kiss. She simply said 'no' and that was that.

The second date started out in front of a shop, because she wanted to meet in a public place, and ended over a bowl of noodles. The third was at the cinema. When she said 'no' for the third time Ennio started thinking that he was never going to get anywhere.

But on the fourth, in a fashionable bar with European music, she let him hold her hand. 'Later we will be able to say that this is where it all started,' she said with a smile, looking around. It was a well-timed comment. Without that encouragement Ennio would have given her the boot, he was so frustrated. As he admired her figure through her tightly fitting clothes he felt like a puppy salivating over a juicy bone.

With Derek away, he was able to invite guests back to the apartment. On their fifth date she agreed to meet him there. As they lay on the bed, he kept his hands under his head to prevent himself from grabbing her behind. She lay to his side with her arms crossed, leaning her chest lightly on his.

She looked into his eyes. Without words they played the let's-see-who-blinks-first game. 'I won!' she said with glee, and then a few moments later: 'This all seems like a dream.'

The sweetness of these words pierced the Italian's cold, bitter, dried up heart. She thought he was her knight in shining armour. 'You'll have to kick me out,' she said, which he knew meant that she was going to stay the night.

But even then she didn't give herself up completely. Ennio had to make do with her hand. She took off her dress and slipped under the covers. He started to feel her leg, but she said, 'you're not going to take advantage of me, are you?'

'Of course not,' he replied, biting his tongue. He turned his back on her and fell asleep.

This, it turned out, was the final test. A few minutes later she was nibbling at his ear. 'I woke you up!' she said teasingly as she got out of bed to go to the bathroom.

Ennio recognised this new sign. While she was out of the room he pulled down his shorts, and when she got back under the covers he started to rub it up against her. She let him kiss her but otherwise didn't react, as if a little scared. So he pulled her hand down between his legs, and she gave him what he would boast to his friends was 'the best hand job I've ever had'.

Playing the prude, she still wouldn't let herself be undressed completely. Later that night he woke her for more hand relief. He squatted over her as she pulled with both hands. She averted her eyes as he squirted his liquid. Some of it landed on her ear.

Michelle was the first woman Ennio wanted to have sex with more than once, and he soon became bewitched. As she became more comfortable she revealed a repertoire of bedtime tricks. Her experience was a little disconcerting, but the pleasure was such that this detail was overlooked. When they kissed she flicked her tongue around in his mouth as if it were a flame.

It wasn't only the sex. Ennio was in awe of Michelle's sensuality too, her movements, her giggles, the way she lit her cigarettes. He was impressed by the variety of her outfits. He thought she must have borrowed from friends, as it was at least a month before he saw her wear the same outfit twice.

He was enchanted, in love. Getting married was the only way he could think of owning her, of keeping her to himself. 'She is an angel sent down from heaven just for me,' he told his colleagues. 'A real woman, perfect.'

He spent three months' earnings on a ring. She said yes on condition they went that night to tell her mother. They agreed upon a quick, simple ceremony. Almost all the guests were her relatives, plus half a dozen hacks not in the field.

Things started to go wrong more or less as soon as he said 'I do'.

To start with, he began to feel uncouth, a loafer. Michelle was prim and proper, educated at the best schools. Ennio, despite his move up in the world, was still a boy from the Abruzzo.

But most importantly, he couldn't handle her jealousy. Whenever he went on a job she became convinced he was seeing another woman. She invented stories, pulled together wild fantasies and worked on theoretical flings with women he knew. These flings might well have taken place had he not been head-over-heels. Ironically, he never thought of touching another woman.

Michelle also became convinced Ennio would die, making her the next name on the long list of Saigon widows. She immediately started putting pressure on him to give up the job and take her to Europe.

Ennio's schedule and his line of work was no help. Life was pretty dicey. Not getting shot by US choppers was in itself an achievement. And once you were in one it was quite likely you would get shot down. Chopper pilots were among the bravest men in the war.

Michelle became so worried she would physically try to prevent Ennio leaving for work. She would scratch his face, forcing him to pretend he had a pet cat.

Photographers like Ennio were 'buying it' all the time. *Life* photographer Larry Burrows lost his life over Laos. Several times when Ennio failed to report in after a crash-landing, both Michelle and Derek were convinced he was dead. It would sometimes take him days to get back in touch. The only way friends and relatives could be sure there was a chance someone was alive was to check the casualty list.

Fully aware that a gay husband was even more of a problem than a female lover, Ennio gave only cursory details about Derek and their 'friendship'. Unsure at the same time of how Derek would react, he didn't inform his friend about the wedding.

Inevitably Derek heard soon after returning to Vietnam. When he realised he was back in town, Ennio did what he could to keep his wife at a safe distance. When Derek wandered over in a restaurant looking to be introduced, Ennio waved him away. When Ennio saw Derek coming down the street he turned the other way, telling Michelle he had forgotten something and needed to go back to the house.

Ennio felt guilty about betraying his only real friend, but told himself he had no choice. If Michelle told her father about a suspicious relationship with another man, the matter might be settled with a bullet.

A couple of weeks into this charade, Derek came around to Ennio's new luxury apartment looking for an explanation. Ennio came to the door wearing nothing but a towel covering his hard-on. This was for Derek the final insult. He knocked Ennio to the ground with a right hook and walked off. To Michelle, to explain the bruising, Ennio made up a story about a fight over money.

She found out, of course. People talked. This sparked off probing questions at first. Then she stopped trying to hide her suspicions. When Ennio eventually invited Derek around for dinner (the two could never stay apart for long) Michelle made a comment about having to leave for the evening and said on the way out: 'I'll leave you two alone. I suppose I'll have to change the sheets now.'

Almost everyone in Saigon knew about Derek and Ennio. Hiding his past from Michelle became impossible. The damage was already done.

Part Four

Quang Tri was a new apex in Ennio's career. It was a double triumph in the true tradition of the photo-reporter.

As a reporter he scooped everyone on the town's fall, a major embarrassment for both the Americans and the South Vietnamese. The story he phoned in from amid the rubble made the front page of *Le Monde* and was followed up all over the world.

As a photographer he took some of his best shots of peasants killed in an ambush, their body-parts partially submerged in sand dunes just outside town. The photos, critics said, turned corpses into elegant, poignant figures. It was as if they were drowning in the sand; in one case you could see only a hand sticking out.

Impressed by his camera equipment, a scooter-borne student gave Ennio a lift. Without this ride he may well have numbered among the many Quang Tri victims, because the town's American 'advisors' wanted him dead.

His protectors, the Americans, were by this time nervous and suspicious of anyone. Around eighty advisors had been unable to flee ahead of Quang Tri's fall. Two caught Ennio dictating copy from a brown army phone found by pure chance among the ruins. It was in one of the few houses left standing.

All those still alive were fleeing the approaching mortar shells, but despite efforts to slip away from the frightened pack, the two officers saw him duck into the building. He was amazed that the line was still open. One army base patched him through to another, and within a couple of minutes he was in contact with the Agence France Presse office in Saigon.

He simply told them what he had seen: 'The South Vietnamese have given up their command post… The town has been abandoned. The VC are inside the town perimeter… The South Vietnamese are too busy retreating to fire their machine guns… The attack helicopters can't provide any more relief… Two were shot down while trying to reach American advisors holed up in their headquarters…'

It was a dispassionate report. 'There are fires everywhere and it's difficult to see more than twenty metres… The locals are running for their lives, carrying fans and televisions… Many have been killed by shrapnel… Some are lying on the ground, alive, but unable to walk… A small black and white dog has followed me part of the way, wounded too and crying… There are broken tanks in the street and overturned jeeps everywhere… It is impossible to drive down many of the streets because trees and telephone wires have fallen in the way…'

He thought he had given the Americans the slip, but they came back looking for him and found him on the phone. One pointed a finger at Ennio and said something he didn't catch. Noting the fear and anger in their faces, he decided it was not a good moment for explanations. The men began shouting. One pulled a gun. Ennio ran, leaving the house through a hole in the wall and then hiding behind heaps of rubbish. From there he ran again in spurts, zig-zagging to make it harder for anyone to take pot shots at him.

The lift from the student was greeted as a gift from God. She looked at his cameras and then glanced at the back of her scooter, indicating that he should mount.

They drove straight into the carnage. The fleeing population of Quang Tri went south into sand dunes. The North Vietnamese hid behind the dunes and opened up when they were close enough. When the scooter arrived the sand was already starting to cover the bodies like a blanket, as if it were a natural burial.

He bought the scooter from the student for a handful of banknotes and drove straight back along jungle tracks, crossing several enemy lines, to Saigon and to a hero's welcome from the press pack.

When the news report appeared in *Le Monde*, the Saigon authorities wanted Ennio out of the country. They raided his apartment and found a selection of military hardware, including grenades and AK47s. Most reporters had similar mementos, the spoils of war. An arrest warrant was put out for unauthorised possession of arms. Ennio was suspected, the warrant said, of being a 'subversive'.

The search party almost found him two days later in a restaurant; he was tipped off just in time and hid under the table. After this, he decided to lie low, staying with friends and colleagues for a few nights at a time.

After three weeks it was Derek's turn to hide 'the subversive'. This meant giving in to Derek's insistence, but Ennio decided this was better than being carted off by the military police for a certain beating. A few days later, when other priorities imposed, the police stopped looking for him.

'Do you remember Gordon Snell's bottle party?' Derek said when they were in bed. 'You were objecting that I was asking you for the moon in the well, when I said you could become a journalist too?'

'Yes, so what?'

'Well, don't you realise that in Quang Tri, you got hold of the moon with your hands and brought it up out of the well? It was brilliant. Signor Iacobucci, you've astounded us all! I'll soon be calling you the man-with-the-moon.'

''What bullshit!' said Ennio, clearly delighted.

Ennio's images had captivated the world, but the Vietnam War was within months to be symbolised by another shot taken by a competitor. Huynh Cong Ut, better known as Nick, from the US agency Associated Press, took the image of the nine-year-old girl, Phan Thi Phuc, running naked on the road. She had shed her smouldering clothes set alight by the napalm dropped on her village.

Ennio did indeed hold the moon in his hands. From total obscurity he had within a few years of meeting Derek become a world-famous, feted, war photographer. Strangers pointed to him in restaurants. Women he had never met before flirted openly with him. Editors of major publications cold-called him and apologised for the intrusion.

But as soon as the war was over and his job done, he was quickly forgotten.

*

From the moment Henry Kissinger arrived in Vietnam, things began to move fast. The Americans' time was coming to an end, and so was Ennio's, he knew.

With Kissinger's arrival began a whirlwind of talks and secret negotiations about withdrawal and ceasefire, accompanied by accusations of betrayal.

Ennio stopped following. He didn't care. All he knew was that the Americans were leaving him, and that Michelle was threatening to do the same. In his desperation to keep her he threw yet more money into the perfume business, even travelling to Hong Kong to buy the latest beauty products. When this wasn't enough to placate her, he agreed to her demand that she be allowed to attend a course in beauty therapy in Paris.

Pushing to the back of his mind the anxiety over what he would do when the Americans were gone, he threw himself into his work. Rather than go out into the field he took shots of daily life in Saigon, of street children selling newspapers, stealing, shining shoes. 'Why feel sorry for these brats?' he thought. All of us have it within ourselves to change our lives for the better.

Michelle returned from France but their relationship did not improve. She shut herself in their apartment and refused to come to the door.

'I'll kill you and your entire family unless you open up right now,' Ennio shouted through the letterbox.

'If she keeps humiliating me, I'll carry out my threat,' he told a friend. 'She won't even let me into my own house. How can a woman who weighs just sixty kilos ruin your life?'

On March 29, 1973 Ennio covered the withdrawal of the American army. It was a low-key event, and nobody could understand why he was crying. At the Tan Son Nhut airbase an American Starfighter transport plane parked in a corner of the runway and the last depressed-looking American soldiers got on board. As they did, Vietcong officers, some in bare feet, tapped them on the shoulder and ticked them off on a clipboard as if they were cattle. The troops walked on board with their heads down like prisoners. Ennio took a picture of every passenger, and not one was smiling. The last soldier on board was General Weyland. He did not shake hands or salute the Vietcong.

It was a waste of time. No-one bought the photos.

The real drama, and the images that defined the withdrawal, took place two years later. The American ambassador, who bizarrely hung on until the last minute, was evacuated in a small fleet of helicopters from rooftops in Saigon while hysterical Vietnamese mobbed the embassy. This retreat for many symbolised the American surrender to the Communists.

Ennio had become so used to the American presence he couldn't imagine Vietnam without them. 'I loved them, but they deserted me,' he said. 'Once more, I am alone.'

The impression the Americans had made was greater than he realised. Without knowing it he had picked up all the American jargon. It was only after Vietnam that he discovered 'R and R' was not a common term for holiday everywhere else in the English-speaking world. And that a 'bird' was not a regular synonym for a helicopter.

The shock of the pullout of the army was compounded by his domestic disasters. The perfume salon was deep in debt. Michelle, who by this time owed her husband thousands of dollars, began to talk of going back to Paris. Ennio told her he wanted the money back before she left, but when he went around to her mother's place to collect, they bolted the doors and pretended not to hear him banging.

Again he considered the Italian solution; wait for the mother and daughter to emerge for dinner and then, 'bang, bang'. Two simple pistol shots and it's all over. He even rehearsed the last lines he would shout as he ended her life.

But all thought of revenge evaporated when he confronted her in a restaurant shortly before she left Saigon for good. 'Listen, I just want you back,' he said hysterically. 'Don't leave me. I'm not gay – you know that. You make me happy. I want to have a son with you.'

It was to no avail. His words of love were drowned out by Michelle's screaming. 'I want a divorce… I don't want a man who's going to be dead tomorrow. If you were a real man, a man who really wanted to be a father, you would find a real job that didn't involve risking your life every day. And what's more, you're a brute. Do you think I like being slapped around?'

‘I didn’t hit you hard,’ Ennio said, pathetically. ‘You wouldn’t shut up.’

‘I hate you,’ she said. ‘I’m going to Paris and I’m never coming back. You’ll never see me again.’

‘You touch another man’s prick and I’ll cut it off in front of you,’ Ennio threatened.

‘Thanks for the passport,’ she said, making for the door. ‘Goodbye Ennio.’

*

Within days of his wife leaving him for good, Ennio was sacked for cowardice.

Depressed and drinking heavily, he reported for work with an agency that had taken him on full-time. He was asked to go to Cai Lay to follow the fighting and refused, saying there was no way he could safely get close enough. His boss overlooked this and instructed him instead to cover an ammunition dump explosion. Ennio refused again, saying he was sick. He was told to go home and not bother coming back.

He had lost his enthusiasm and resented taking orders. He could rely on freelance commissions, he thought.

But at the same time the world’s news services were losing their enthusiasm for Vietnam. Without the US there was no longer a villain to the story. The commissions dried up, and before long Ennio had no income at all.

Derek felt the change in the news agenda too. The BBC, for whom he was now working full time, told him to spend more time working out of Singapore. The rest of Asia was ‘more newsworthy,’ they said. With correspondents leaving Vietnam every month, Ennio soon felt friendless.

Six months later, the Rolex watch had been sold and the reality of Michelle’s abandonment had sunk in. On the night he knew for sure she would never come back, Ennio checked into a Saigon hotel room with a typewriter, a red typewriter ribbon, a bottle of whisky and another, of barbiturates.

He wrote to Derek, in red:

I can’t stand life anymore. I have achieved more or less what I wanted to achieve. I blame no one for my decision. It’s my fault for having been born too sentimental. I'm sorry to leave my dear Mamma. You're also her son as far as she is concerned.

I've never felt so lonely and disappointed in my entire existence. I must blame myself for having been too honest and loyal to everybody. I hoped my marriage would bring me happiness and an heir. I believed in love, but did not find it.

I tried with other women and it didn't work out. I wanted a vendetta, but kept myself under control. I don't want to harm anyone. I only regret my ignorance.

I take away an excellent impression of you. You have a right to my possessions in Italy. I thank you for everything. Until another time and place perhaps? Your exploiter: Ennio.

Ennio knew Derek was in town, and so sent the letter by hand delivery, the address also typed in red ink, to the Reuters office.

Derek put it in his pocket when he received it. He was in the middle of typing up a story on the abandonment of the South Vietnamese by their American allies. Military aid had dried up to a dribble, and while the North Vietnamese built up their forces, the South Vietnamese Army was already rationing shells.

He read the letter back in his hotel. Halfway through he sat on the floor for support.

At the same moment the black pre-war phone rang in his room. There was a woman's voice on the other end. She spoke French.

'This is the Grall Hospital. We have *Monsieur* the Italian photographer here. If *Monsieur* would wish to see him…'

Derek made as if to answer but only a croaking noise came forth.

He tried again: 'Do you mean his body?'

She tut-tutted.

'Oh no Sir. He's quite alive, I would say…'

'Can I come and see him?'

'That's why we phone. He's been asking for you.'

The French-run Grall Hospital was a grandiose place in vast grounds with big airy pavilions separated by lawns, neat flower-beds and shaded walks, a tiny plot of Europe.

The young, bonneted, duty-sister greeted Derek. 'Ennio was found by a young lady lying unconscious on the floor in a cheap hotel with pills scattered everywhere,' she said. 'I understand his wife has left him. He was in a sadly serious state. It is lucky the friend found him when she did.' She smiled. 'Now, happily, he is on the mend.'

The sister took Derek to Ennio's room. He was standing in pyjamas. His eyes moistened when they hugged. He was unable to speak.

'What a bloody, bloody fool you were,' Derek whispered to him. 'Fancy trying to leave me like that. The cheek of it!'

But Ennio was in no mood to be humoured.

'I'm still not sure I want to be here,' he said flatly. 'I can't have locked the door of that hotel room properly. What happens now? I don't know.' He flopped onto the bed and started weeping.

'Can I take him away with me?' Derek asked the sister. She looked at him uncertainly, trying to decide. It was Saturday.

'Well, he's due to be discharged on Monday, so I don't suppose a day less makes that much difference. Mind you, I don't know what Matron will say. You'll have to sign a responsibility form.'

'What about dinner tonight young man?' Derek asked. Ennio nodded vigorously.

Derek waited for him to turn up in the appointed restaurant for a long time before eating alone. On the way home, looking through the window of another well-known eatery, he spotted Ennio chewing away opposite an American correspondent. 'Am I just here to mop up his mess after he leaves?' Derek asked.

The next day he received a summons from the Italian consulate. The Consul General, a woman, was furious.

'You ruined our plans,' she said. 'We were about to have Ennio repatriated on medical grounds. I know him well. He comes often to chat. Didn't you see that he is ill? His state will only worsen if he stays in Saigon. The Ambassador agreed with me, but now that he has been officially discharged from hospital, how can I explain repatriation on medical grounds to the Foreign Ministry in Rome?'

She wagged a pencil in Derek's direction. 'You've created this mess, so it's up to you to undo it.' She handed him a stub of paper. 'It's a free air ticket, valid for a week.'

Derek was not optimistic. It seemed like a hopeless mission. But when he finally tracked Ennio down in one of his watering holes, to his bewilderment no convincing was necessary.

'I'll be using Rome, I think, to cover the Middle East and Latin America,' Ennio proclaimed airily. 'And I'm not even going to ask you for the taxi fare from Rome airport to the city centre. I don't want to be any more trouble to you. I'm determined not to be an exploiter ever again.'

He paused for thought and said, almost to himself: 'The big question is whether I'll be able to re-adapt myself to Italian life. Let us see.'

Several days later, with no fuss or tears, he left on an Air Vietnam flight, destination Rome via Bangkok.

*

At first there was a long silence. It lasted several months. Then the letters began. Each was worse than the last.

I go out very rarely because I can't re-accustom myself to the Italians' mentality and way of life. The people here disgust and sadden me. We Italians are pathetic in the eyes of others. Everything is so disappointing. What do I do? Go back to the quiet country-life again? Impossible. What's the point of living a hundred years waiting for death, counting off the hours with an egg-timer? It's far better to live just a bit of life but to live it really well...

Then another:

I'm alone and lost. The only people I love are two. One is Michelle and in spite of everything I still love her. The second is you, even though there's been nothing between us recently. Apart from you two, there is no-one else and I don't want anybody else... I cannot forget her: I am too much in love. But she left me because she thinks I go to bed with you. She doesn't realise how faithful I have been. I wanted to stay in Asia with you and her. Asia is ideal for me. But now the Americans have left Vietnam, what do I do?

And a third:

I'm living in a world of fantasy because I no longer believe in anything. I have even lost what pride in myself I had. I know I had my chance and have blown it. I've made a mess of my life and know it's too late to start again. The result is a sense of guilt. I see a difficult life ahead, without hope. I know I've left you more than once. But what can I do about it? Regret it? Forget it? It may seem strange after all that's happened, but you're still the only person I live for...

Things started to get ugly for Saigon. Over Christmas of 1974, heavy fighting broke out in an obscure province near the Cambodian border, Phuoc Long. North Vietnamese units overran all five of the province's lesser townships, and only the capital, also called Phuoc Long, was holding out. If that town fell too, it was to be the first time an entire province had been lost to Communist forces since the Americans moved in. US forces were not intervening to punish Hanoi in any way. The Saigon commander told his men they had no alternative but to fight or die since they were local boys.

Derek reported developments by cable.

January 5: Latest reports are of North Vietnamese tanks and infantry again breaking through the defence perimeter. Some 250,000 civilians are said to be trapped...

January 6: The High Command in Saigon reported fires blazing and heavy fighting still in progress at day-break in the besieged provincial capital of Phuoc Long after an all-night battle during which radio contact with headquarters in the town was lost...

Another letter arrived from Rome.

I have nobody but you. Do you want me to come back and live with you? Shall we have another try? I want to leave at once. May I drink to our new life together? What do you say? When we meet, you'll see a new Ennio, the Ennio of years ago, the Ennio you knew in Paris...

On the sixth day of fighting, Phuoc Long fell to the Communists amid reports of heavy civilian casualties. A doom-like atmosphere hung like a cloud over Saigon.

'The Americans have abandoned their allies. They are indifferent,' Derek wrote in his diary. 'I will not do the same. Here is another cry for help. I will not ignore it.' The same night he shot off a cable to

Ennio agreeing to another go at co-existence. But, still smarting from past brush-offs, he added a proviso: 'You must state that you will always be physically available and willing to me.'

Ennio replied: 'What alternative have I?'

Derek sent him a ticket routed to Saigon via Moscow.

*

Ennio's frame of mind did not improve much with his return. When Derek came home one night he found his friend sitting on the sofa, slumped over a bottle. He had broken in to the apartment through the bathroom window. The maid was beside herself with hysteria at the sight of him. 'Ciao,' said Derek, slapping him on the back, but the Italian did not bother to reply.

Derek made him stick to his 'availability' pledge for a few days, after which he was set free. 'He did comply, but with such a theatrical show of being nailed to a cross that my "slave" soon won his liberty,' Derek wrote in his diary.

Ennio's heavy drinking had started to overtake him. He went back to work, but was more often than not sloshed behind the lens.

Everyone was expecting Phuoc Long to be followed up with another attack, possibly in the Highlands, so the photographer went out to scout the region with a new friend he had picked up; a Corsican by the name of Paul Leandri. Paul also worked for Agence France Presse and wore red knee-length boots everywhere he went. Another lover of danger and a risk-taker, he would when travelling in choppers sit on the floor and swing his legs about dangerously in the air.

They came back with photos showing a big South Vietnamese build-up around Pleiku, Hanoi's suspected next target. But weeks later there was still no action.

For Ennio, a freelance, no action meant no sellable pictures, which meant no money. He started mumbling about having made the 'wrong decision' in leaving Rome, and talked of flogging his cameras and going back. He complained about the maid's cooking and accused Derek of being 'careless, egotistical and miserly'. Rumours that Michelle was in town did not help his state of mind. He went looking for her but was turned away by guards armed with machine guns surrounding her family's villa. The perfume salon had closed.

Feeling he was no longer welcome and increasingly reliant on Derek for loans to move around the country, Ennio's moods shuttled between anger and despair. He felt no sympathy for the South Vietnamese now the Americans were gone. He wanted to leave the country for Cambodia, which by this time was also on the brink of a conflagration. 'I want to get in before it's too late,' he said. Derek loaned him fifteen dollars for a one-way ticket.

On Saturdays, the Saigon Government nonsensically allowed the Vietcong to hold a weekly news conference in a compound called Camp Davis, in line with a clause in the albeit dead Peace Agreement. At the last conference before the capital was attacked, journalists turned up as usual to be hectored by Colonel An Giang, as shrivelled and ascetic as a fasting monk. The colonel predicted a 'gathering storm' as punishment for Saigon's (not Hanoi's) arrogant flouting of the Peace Agreement. 'Our forces have gained undeniable superiority,' he said. 'The initiative has passed into our hands.' Halfway through the conference there was the usual interval.

Bizarrely, Ennio then entered the compound and introduced himself to the colonel. He had no interest in words, only in pictures that said what words could not, and so never attended such events. Derek approached the desk where the two were standing and caught the end of their conversation. Ennio said: 'I thought it may interest you,' slipping a document under the colonel's blotter. Looking over Ennio's shoulder, Derek's puzzlement grew when he thought he recognised his own writing in the margins of some typed script.

The colonel raised a finger in acknowledgment, at which Ennio spun round to stand squarely in front of Derek. Without acknowledging his friend, he dog-legged around him and headed for the exit. Derek followed. 'What on earth are you doing Ennio? What was that you gave him?' he asked as they crossed the compound threshold.

'You should know. It was your list,' Ennio said without expression, walking off briskly.

‘List?’ Derek asked. ‘What list?’ He walked to his office, determined to check his files and figure out by process of elimination what was missing.

Before arriving he already suspected. When he opened his filing cabinet, his suspicions were confirmed. Ennio had handed the Vietcong Derek’s ‘Quang file’, named after one of his best contacts. Under the names of all South Vietnamese military bases there were tabulated columns showing the bases’ dwindling supplies, supplies the Americans had failed to replenish. It showed that only ten percent of the Army’s fuel supplies was left. Spare parts for tanks were totally finished. Shell stocks were down fifty-five percent. Only a third of jeeps were serviceable. Only a third of the C130 transport planes were flyable. Soldiers were on patrol, the document showed, with just two grenades each when they should have had ten.

Derek sighed. The next day Ennio was in Phnom Penh. Two days later fighting broke out in Vietnam, not in the Highlands as expected but in the market town of Ban Me Thuot. It was the start of the rout of the South.

*

Soon after landing in Cambodia, Ennio learned of the death of his friend Paul Leandri. It was directly related to the latest fighting.

While the two were scouting around the Highlands, Leandri had looked up a French cleric whom he had quoted anonymously in a story. Leandri wrote that an anti-Saigon Montagnard independence movement called Furlo had shown the North Vietnamese the easiest avenues for their attack on Ban Me Thuot.

The Saigon Immigration Department had summoned Leandri to their offices, wanting the priest’s name. He refused. Hoping he would cave in, they kept him alone in an office. He smashed furniture, shouting in protest. So they led him to a pebbled forecourt and left him there. He began pacing up and down ever more hurriedly, shouting to himself. Then he attempted an escape. He made it as far as the agency’s Peugeot and angrily skidded off at full throttle, churning up a wake of pebbles. Guards lunging for the door-handles were flung to the ground. The Peugeot smashed through the single-rod barrier into the boulevard past sentries with raised rifles. One round tore through the closed driver's window into Leandri's skull.

Knowing how the news would affect Ennio and determined to confront him over his treachery at the Vietcong press conference, Derek took the next plane to the Cambodian capital, much to the annoyance of the BBC, whose editors resented this shipping out just as things were hotting up for Saigon.

As expected, he found Ennio slumped over a drink in the hotel bar.

'They've killed Leandri,' Ennio muttered. 'The staff at the French Embassy will start pulling out tomorrow. I'm going to cover the story and I'm going to get myself killed as well, by a Khmer Rouge mortar.'

'One impulse shouldn't lead to another,' said Derek.

'I never knew I could hate you so much,' Ennio told him.

'Why did you pass on Quang's notes to the Vietcong?' Derek asked.

'I can't find her!' Ennio sobbed and shouted. 'She's left me! She's gone! What do you expect me to do? It's what they deserve!'

'I thought it might be something like that,' said Derek. 'However, I doubt you've changed the course of the war at this late stage.'

Ennio wasn't listening. 'I know I've made mistakes,' he said. 'I've let myself be influenced by people too much. Trouble is, I wasn't capable of taking the decisions I should have. You've made something of your life. What have I done? A mess! I'm a failure. I wanted to stay quietly in Asia with my adored Michelle and you. But now I've no work and no money and everybody is leaving me, dear Michelle, then Leandri, and you're off now, too.'

The next day Derek took a Caravelle back to Saigon. Through a plane port-hole he watched Ennio darting about on the tarmac without helmet or flak-jacket, snapping French diplomats running for a French military jet.

*

Ennio was one of the few photographers left to record the fall of Phnom Penh on April 17, 1975. The work he sent on a spool on the last plane out of the capital ended up splashed all over the *New York Times*, which nominated him for a Pulitzer Prize.

He took shots of the child-size Khmer Rouge soldiers in baggy black shirts, smiling under caps, with check scarves around their necks and dwarfed by the grenade launchers on their backs, marching in. They marched straight down the capital's main thoroughfare, Monivong Boulevard.

People came out to cheer them, thinking the end of the war had come at last. And then they took a second look, their smiles fading as the soldiers un-holstered their pistols. The boys began firing into the air and the people fled. They were occupiers, not liberators.

In other pictures, the advancing bands of barelegged youths were disciplined and unsmiling. Some government soldiers abandoned their weapons; others changed their uniforms for black, Communist pyjamas. The navy signalled surrender with a continuous blast of sirens from the river fleet.

It was dangerous work, but Ennio kept carefully concealed. Hiding in doorways, behind tree trunks, in empty upstairs flats or abandoned taxis to take his pictures, he tracked the country's new masters, followed them right into the heart of the city. There was firing everywhere. The Khmer Rouge was going door-to-door, ordering people to evacuate the city and to leave all their possessions behind. They even forced patients out of the hospitals. Some were pushed along in their beds, looking like they were just out of the operating theatre.

When they reached the town centre Ennio and two other journalists took refuge in Le Phnom hotel, but after a few hours the Khmer Rouge announced it was no longer a protected area and moved them off to the French embassy, where one or two diplomats, including the consul, were still in residence. Thousands of those who had supported the old regime, a whole range of nationalities, soon converged on the embassy, desperate for some kind of protection.

The new Phnom Penh authorities surrounded the embassy, one of the only foreign presences they respected.

Inside, people at first wandered around as if hypnotised. There was little to do other than sunbathe and wait for the end to come. Ennio spent much of the time frying in his trunks by the empty swimming pool.

From outside the embassy perimeter began to waft a putrid smell. The killing had begun, a massacre that would end the lives of one Cambodian in three.

Desperation levels mounted. Politicians arrived asking for asylum, including the former prime minister, Sirik Matak. Everyone wanted to save his own skin and to hell with everyone else.

Within days the Khmer Rouge 'invited' the French Consul to draw up a list of all those inside. All Cambodians were ordered to leave. Stories circulated of rape, burning and summary execution. Shots could be heard coming from the streets just beyond the perimeter.

The Consul advised everyone to flee before the embassy was searched, but no-one knew where to go. A few days later, Matak and the former president of the national assembly, both of whom figured on the list of Khmer Rouge enemies due for immediate, summary execution, handed themselves in.

The remaining Cambodians, many in tears, prepared to leave and face their grim fate. Only one local girl remained after convincing a French journalist to marry her. After the departures around 600 were left in the embassy. Food and water quickly ran out. Two days later, illness appeared, hundreds of cases of dysentery.

After two weeks holed up in the compound the embassy received orders that all foreigners were to be evacuated to Thailand. The ragged bunch of survivors were lined up at dawn and packed into open trucks. In Ennio's there were twenty-five people.

They were shipped across devastated countryside and all wondered if they would ever get to the Thai border, a four-day trip. The convoy got lost several times and got stuck even more often when the trucks ran into bomb holes in the roads. Passengers fought each other over food. Ennio hit a little French man after he took rice from his plate. After three days people were so edgy a riot was close to breaking out. A baby died en route.

Ennio left Indochina as a refugee. It was his curtain call; he would never return. It was seven years since he'd first arrived in Saigon.

His disturbing studies of the brain-washed, under-age Khmer Rouge automatons also made the *Sunday Times* in London alongside a piece by Jon Swain, a piece that won Swain Britain's Reporter of the Year award.

*

From Thailand Ennio travelled to Singapore, where he stayed with Derek. Coming down from the war was a shock for both men. All the work they were offered was boring, beneath them. 'After Vietnam, we were both Gullivers surrounded around our feet by townsfolk too small to see,' wrote Derek in his autobiography. 'We had witnessed what they never could. It was not arrogance but sudden loneliness. The trivialities that concerned those around us were almost comic… We were mentally on the dole because there was no challenge for supermen.'

To relieve the boredom they drank too much in freezing hotel bars. They had frequent tiffs over nothing. Off Malaysia, on the island of Penang, their base for overseeing the Malaysian army's efforts to root out the last of the Chinese Communist guerrillas, in the 'Lone Pine' hotel, they argued over the waiter, the service, the bill. Derek stormed off and drove home alone, branding Ennio a 'drunken peasant'.

Back in Singapore they spent one Sunday night watching a film at the Tanglin Club, a gilded retreat for resident expatriates. Ennio was driving and twice missed the concealed pebbled entranceway. 'Are you stupid or something?' barked Derek, at which Ennio braked hard, got out of the car and walked away.

Another night, at the Holiday Inn, both men were sat at the bar without speaking, staring into the mirror behind the bottles. Ennio was given gin and tonic with no lemon. He exploded: 'These stupid British! I wish they would kick them out! They deserve it. They are so stupid. They don't understand the Asian mentality. It's a Mafia. I'm anti-British. You're like them…'

After a few weeks Derek got a call to cover a hostage crisis; the Japanese Red Army had occupied the American consulate in Kuala Lumpur. He was grateful for the chance to leave.

Ennio considered asking to travel with him, but didn't. He stayed in Singapore a little longer, wallowing in his personal loss. A week later, he took a plane to Rome.

Alone. The nightmares returned. Another letter:

I want to thank you for your hospitality and kindness in Singapore. Our separation was too quick, unexpected. I should have come with you. I could have sold a lot of photos. After a few days back in Italy, the nightmares, the apprehension have returned. Things are worse than ever. My sister has been screaming at me for leaving the cupboards open and my things lying around the house. My mother only cares about what and how much I am eating. I have lost touch with everyone. Why do I let myself get depressed so easily? Am I too sensitive? Too weak? You know, I miss you a tremendous amount and I don't know what to do without you. You'll no doubt tell me to go to hell, but what I say is true. It's just that when I have you in front of me, I never manage to express my feelings or thoughts. I don't think my life will be very interesting without you. I meant to tell you, but you were in a hurry to leave. It's not life I'm afraid of; it's solitude and boredom. I've avoided people up to now, because I wasn't ready, but obviously I've got to face the jungle soon... I embrace you with a kiss. Ever yours, Ennio.

He made efforts to keep his career on track. He travelled to Lisbon to cover the aftermath of the military coup against the dictatorship, though the lack of fighting meant he barely covered his costs with the few pictures he sold. He made plans for a trip to Angola, and a book on Vietnam.

But things did not turn out as planned. He returned empty-handed from Israel, where he had been sent to take photos of politicians. He couldn't find a way to get anywhere near them. After this debacle, the commissions dried up completely. He was struck by the irony: it was in Israel his career began. 'Will Israel be the end of my career, too?' he asked himself.

Derek was by this time tired of Ennio's emotional dependence. Out of the blue he was offered the chance to become the BBC Latin America correspondent. He jumped at it, cabling his bosses that he would be 'delighted' to accept, happy that Buenos Aires, his new base, would be so far away from the clingy Italian.

On his way down to the southern hemisphere, Derek stopped off in Rome to tie up loose ends. The two met briefly. Ennio, grasping at the vestiges of his pride, showed Derek a scrapbook of cuttings he had put together in preparation for his novel. 'I don't know when

I'm going to have time to dedicate to it, what with all this travel,' he said. Neither man brought up the subject of their relationship.

'He struck me as reasonably happy with his work and was looking well,' Derek wrote in his diary, adding that this was 'the practical end of our long relationship'.

Derek left Rome by train for the airport without inviting Ennio to follow him down to Argentina. At the station, Ennio waved him off. Derek gave a theatrical wave back before slumping down in his carriage, relieved to have left town without having to suffer yet another hysterical scene.

Ennio's bravado and talk of ongoing projects hid a different reality, a redundant reality. 'Rome is not Vietnam, young man,' said the American correspondents re-posted to Italy after the war. 'Sorry, Ennio, there's nothing for you here.' Despite the knock-backs he continued to tour the offices, and soon the press pack was sick of his pleading.

Four more months passed. He sent Derek a birthday greeting. 'If I were in Buenos Aires now, I would be able to invite you to dinner for your birthday,' the letter started.

Next year, I hope. In fact, the main news for you is that I'm putting a bit of money aside to be able to come to Buenos Aires. If I come, will you be there? If not, where will I find you? Let me know. I hope I'll be able to work, even as a waiter. Will you be glad if I come? I would like to stay in Argentina three years, if not more. I'm contacting newspapers in Rome and Milan and they are all eager. Will you be able to put me up if I come? I could be your secretary. Please let me know something as quickly as you can.

I have tried finding work and setting myself up in Rome, but it is impossible. My Italian competitors, the scum, are envious of my Vietnam reputation. I know they are keeping me in the dark whenever there is a job going. I did get offered one job, at the Durazzi agency. But it was a mistake. I realised the other partners were beginners, the wrong type of people. So I left. Being fully freelance is best.

I have always worked better abroad. A lot of things are not working out, including on a psychological level. I could work for Time *again and the other magazines. In two words, I want to work together with you. Mamma sends you all the best. With affection,* comme toujours, *Ennio.*

Derek took a month to reply. His letter, sent via *Newsweek* in the US, was designed to be off-putting while not shutting the door completely. 'It would be very difficult for you to work under a military regime, more so than in Vietnam, because in Vietnam we were protected by the Americans,' he wrote. 'To be frank, Argentina is no place for you. There is a lot of talk over here about 'sexual deviants,' whatever they are. They are trying to get me out, to force me to leave Argentina. And in any case, doesn't each of us need to run his own life? That said, if you need somewhere to stay, my door is always open.'

It was no exaggeration. Derek had already spent a night in the police station cells after being rounded up with fellow drinkers in a gay bar. Before his release he was informed he had been 'rescued'. The Argentine regime thought of Europeans as deviants. They believed they were the last bastion of civilisation. The British embassy was already beating off requests for Derek's repatriation.

Ennio's reply came quickly.

Your letter has greatly discouraged me. Both the tone of your reply, and the possibility of working under a military regime. But remember how in Vietnam we worked under a military regime? Surely there must be photo agencies in Argentina that need material? But that's my idea. I can only tell you that I don't see much of a future here.

Some of the things you wrote made me think, and it's right each of us runs his own life. But I see your letter as not very inviting. Anyway I want to thank you all the same for your offer of hospitality in case I come out. At least I know I'll have a base to work from, a starting point, and that in itself is a lot. But I haven't taken any decision. Before getting your letter, I was almost sure. But I'll write to you as soon as I know what I'll be up to.

Whatever happens, I don't think I'll stay in Italy, unless I change my job. Because I'm just not prepared to go on counting the pennies every day, with the fear of waking up one fine morning to find I haven't a lira left. That's why I haven't got a flat of my own. It would add to the expense. Now I hope to work a bit more because of early elections though I don't count on them to make a fortune. Our trade is a jungle, too full of trickery. If you know how to lick arses, you can get on. I'm not up to it. I've tried but couldn't do it.

And you? How are you getting on? You must be very involved in work. Strange though, the papers here hardly reported the coup. Are there Italian journalists there?

As for my other problems, I'll tell you about them when I come, if I come, because I'm afraid of boring you if I write about them. I'll send you another letter to let you know how things are going. In the meantime, big best wishes and more than that. Ennio, always.

And then, nothing. Derek was torn between a desire to see him again and what he thought was a need to break away definitively. He wrote a couple more times but received no reply. He was half-expecting to be called back to London to take part in a BBC end-of-year review, and wrote to his friend the Countess informing her he might be in Rome for Christmas. When Ennio's absence continued, he phoned the Countess to ask if she had heard any news.

'Yes, he was here just the other day,' she said. 'He's hit the bottle I'm afraid. He downed drink after drink right here in front of me, and never accepted a sandwich. Not one. He says he's been trying to reach you on the phone.'

That was quite possible, Derek told her. Like many of those lucky enough to have a telephone line in Buenos Aires, he was constantly plagued by crossed lines and wrong numbers at home. He had taken to lifting the receiver, screaming '*equivocado*' and slamming it down before he had heard who was on the other end. He took care of any important messages via cable.

With his family, Ennio kept up appearances. But secretly, meticulously, and with a certain amount of malice, he was planning his suicide. He began by leaving equivocal messages with his friends. He talked to some people of 'a long trip to Africa'.

'Do you want to go out for lunch?' he asked one American correspondent.

'I can't, I'm going skiing tomorrow and I've got to prepare my suitcase,' came the reply over the telephone.

'Too bad, as you won't see me again,' said Ennio.

'What do you mean?'

'I'm going on a long trip to Africa.'

Twice a week he could be found eating alone in his favourite restaurant, Rome's only Vietnamese restaurant, bitterly lecturing the owner about 'that bastard' Kissinger and provoking sympathy with an invented story about his much-loved wife dying during the war in Saigon. They would invariably have to put him in a taxi, blind drunk.

He gave away his four cameras to his brother Graziano. He said he had bought new ones he kept in his office. Over a liquid lunch he'd dropped another hint.

'If you keep up that intake, you'll be dead in your forties,' Graziano had said, watching his drinking.

'I won't make forty.'

'What? Have you made a pact with the Man Upstairs?'

He bought a length of rope, painstakingly winding one end of it with scotch tape so the noose would run. In the lavatory of a garage being built under the dining room of his family's Rome apartment, he fixed the rope to a stout hook screwed into the ceiling. Then he piled six bricks in the shape of a cone on top of a petrol drum. Next to it was a chair from which to step onto the cone.

Two weeks later he drank a flask of wine as he played cards with his mother and sister. As the bottle emptied, he made little jokes that made the two women titter. At the end of the game he laughed and clapped his hands, telling his mother: 'You've won! You've won!' He kissed her on the crown of the head and left the room grinning, saying he was popping out to buy cigarettes.

Downstairs, he smoked a last cigarette before stepping up onto the chair. Above, through the ceiling, he heard his mother's voice just feet away.

As he climbed onto the bricks and placed the noose over his neck while humming Cavaradossi's lines *'L'ora e fuggita e muoio disperato'* (The time is up, I die in despair) he took a swig of wine and wiped his lips with the back of his hand. His brain swam forward slowly as he became Cavaradossi himself, out there on the huge stage, lifting his voice above the surging music before an audience already shedding tears. In his head he heard the wrenching prelude to '*muoio*'. Utter relish at his own doom brought him searing satisfaction, sweetened by the grandiose drama of the tenor's last instants. He pitied all those too gutless to effect a similar exit. He had lived the only essence of life worth living for – and that was love – and he was throwing the rest of it away, like rotten fruit. He was about to face the heartless firing squad of life.

Who was the coward now? In the private theatre of his mind, he was about to die a splendid death. As he hummed the aria for the last time he was more convinced with every note that all those who were close to him deserved what was coming: Derek for his abandonment; his mother for giving him a lousy childhood. Pleased with his logic, he kicked the cone away.

Derek heard the news via the Reuters agency.

Reuters, Rome, Jan 8, 1977: War photographer Ennio Iacobucci, best known for his work in Vietnam and Cambodia, has committed suicide at his home here, police said. Signor Iacobucci, who spent six years in Vietnam, working for Italian television, the New York Times and Newsweek, hanged himself in the basement of his home, where he lived with his mother and sister, police said. Friends said Signor Iacobucci, 35, had been depressed since returning to Italy from southeast Asia about a year ago. For the Italian news photographers' association his was the 'tragic image of a war photographer'. New York Times correspondent Alvin Shuster said: 'He was an excellent photographer who found trouble adjusting to the slow pace of Italy after his long, active and dangerous years in Asia.'

Months later Derek visited Ennio's family and discovered he had been left a note. The envelope had been opened by the police. The note read:

Well, here I am, on my way. If there's a tomorrow, I'll be there. I was born both too fortunate and too unfortunate. I was ambitious and still am. But because of my modesty, I could not find success. Whose fault it is I don't know. I needed you but you were too wrapped up in your silence. I'm glad everything will soon be over. I would have liked to say more seeing you're the only one who understands me, but, alas, you're too far away. I tried phoning you for five days, but without any reply. The minutes I am about to pass through will be ferocious and terrible, but it's better to finish like this. I hope you understand. If there's a tomorrow, you'll always be welcome.

See you soon. Ennio.

Postscript

Brussels, 2010:

Considering that he had a long, successful career as a journalist, it was something of a surprise to read Derek Wilson's draft autobiography and discover he had missed The Story. While his own life was without doubt exceptional and action-packed, it was the tale of his 'lover' Ennio that really grabbed the reader's attention.

Derek was a war correspondent for many years, and knew Europe, Asia, Africa and South America like few others. He was also a big drinker, a lover of life in the fast lane, and a stalwart believer in an objective truth. His obituary in the London *Times* was well deserved.

Written by a good friend, the BBC journalist Brian Barron, the obituary originally contained a reference to Derek's homosexuality and the suicide of his one 'true love', though mysteriously this was edited out prior to publication.

It's a shame, because this love, or obsession, with Ennio, and its tragic conclusion was still ricocheting through Derek's life when I met him in 1991. It was central to his character.

Over many dinners and several years it became apparent that Derek's need for atonement was the main driving factor behind his autobiography. He blamed himself for abandoning Ennio and came up with several theories to explain the desperation that drove him to take his life.

His favourite theory was based loosely on class. One should not attempt to lift anyone above their natural station, he concluded. Ennio was a poor, humble boy, and it was wrong to look to create a sophisticated photographer out of him.

The ten years that followed Ennio's suicide were 'hell', Derek told me in 2007, shortly before he died of heart failure, aged 72. He was referring to a period before I knew him, a period which must indeed have been grim given that much later he was still attempting to undo what he thought he had done. His guilt led to masochistic relationships with Italian boys, sometimes prostitutes.

He entitled his autobiography 'Rich villains, poor villains' after Shakespeare's quote 'When rich villains have need of poor ones, poor ones may take what price they will'. Derek was in his own mind the rich villain (rich compared to Ennio, at any rate), the BBC journalist who selfishly took a young naïve boy and abused him, as many others had done.

Ennio's suicide and the decades of angst that followed were the price he paid, or so he believed. Derek's autobiography was a long apology and an attempt to come to grips with what went wrong, based largely on the diaries he kept over thirty years.

Journalists can get too close to their story; they are sometimes so involved in what they are writing that they fail to see the big picture or to state the obvious. Derek had, I told him, overlooked what he had witnessed first-hand: Ennio's life, the pig boy who made fun of generals, an Italian Dick Whittington with a dark, depressing twist. He was the boy who grabbed the moon at the bottom of the well.

Whereas Derek's life had a certain inevitability to it: Oxford, Reuters, the BBC, Ennio on the other hand was plucked from literally nowhere and thrust into a whirlwind of terror and excitement few can imagine. He went from cleaning shoes to taking photos for the world's most prestigious publications – what a transformation! What on earth went through his mind?

Happily, we do know to a certain extent what made him tick. At the age of twenty, while living here in Brussels, Ennio wrote his own autobiography covering the time from his birth to his arrival in Rome. He never showed it to anyone. Derek read it only after Ennio's suicide.

The wonky, typed notes are repetitive and difficult to decipher but give a haunting insight into a cursed life in the unforgiving Abruzzo mountains, a life that must have left Ennio indelibly marked. He was abandoned by both parents and became a slave in a monastery.

After reading them I told Derek he was surely not to blame for Ennio's final decision; psychologically speaking, Ennio could surely never have seriously hoped to escape his childhood.

Derek initially accepted my suggestion that he change tack, that he re-write his book with a new focus on Ennio. But he later changed his mind and seemed determined to write a set of traditional memoirs. The book would be his swan song, he thought; his final story, all of it fact.

Later still, less than a year before he died, he came around to my new suggestion that I be allowed to tell Ennio's story by combining the Italian's firsthand account with excerpts from Derek's recollections. He sent me both autobiographies and gave me his blessing. 'I feel duty-bound to get the story read in any way,' he said.

This book is therefore to a large extent a selective translation of Ennio's early autobiography, notes and letters tacked onto a re-write of Derek's. I have tried to be consistent in style and character, though I seem to have unwittingly come up with an exercise in misogyny.

Ennio might not come across as all that likeable, though to my mind he was a victim of unusual circumstances. Derek fell for him, tried to help him, but got dragged down when Ennio's childhood caught up with them both.

It is a fatalistic tale, I can't help thinking. No-one was to blame.

#

www.ingramcontent.com/pod-product-compliance
Lightning Source LLC
LaVergne TN
LVHW050647100826
845148LV00011B/2023

9780956368652